PRACTICING TO TAKE THE

GRE®

COMPUTER SCIENCE TEST

2nd Edition

S0-BJK-174

INCLUDES:

- An actual GRE Computer Science Test administered in 1990-91
- Sample questions, instructions, and answer sheets
- Percent of examinees answering each question correctly

AN OFFICIAL PUBLICATION OF THE GRE BOARD

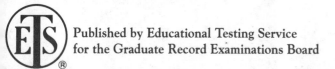

Published by Educational Testing Service
for the Graduate Record Examinations Board

The Graduate Record Examinations Program offers a General Test measuring developed verbal, quantitative, and analytical abilities and Subject Tests measuring achievement in the following 16 fields:

Biochemistry, Cell and Molecular Biology	Economics	Literature in English	Political Science
Biology	Education	Mathematics	Psychology
Chemistry	Engineering	Music	Sociology
Computer Science	Geology	Physics	
	History		

The tests are administered by Educational Testing Service under policies determined by the Graduate Record Examinations Board, an independent board affiliated with the Association of Graduate Schools and the Council of Graduate Schools.

The Graduate Record Examinations Board has officially made available for purchase practice books, each containing a full-length test, for 15 of the Subject Tests. A practice book is not available for the Biochemistry, Cell and Molecular Biology Test at this time. Two General Test practice books are also available. You may purchase these practice books by using the order form on page 87.

Individual booklets describing each test and including sample questions are available free of charge for all 16 Subject Tests. You may request these booklets by writing to:

Graduate Record Examinations
Educational Testing Service
P.O. Box 6014
Princeton, NJ 08541-6014

The Graduate Record Examinations Board and Educational Testing Service are dedicated
to the principle of equal opportunity, and their programs, services, and employment policies
are guided by that principle.

GRE, ETS, EDUCATIONAL TESTING SERVICE, and the ETS logo design are registered trademarks
of Educational Testing Service, registered in the U.S.A. and in many other countries.
GRADUATE RECORD EXAMINATIONS is a U.S. registered trademark of Educational Testing Service.

In association with Warner Books, Inc., a Warner Communications Company.

Copyright © 1991 by Educational Testing Service. All rights reserved.

USA: 0-446-39308-8
CAN: 0-446-39309-6

TABLE OF CONTENTS

BACKGROUND FOR THE TEST

TAKING THE TEST

BACKGROUND FOR THE TEST

PRACTICING TO TAKE THE GRE® COMPUTER SCIENCE TEST

This practice book has been published on behalf of the Graduate Record Examinations Board to help potential graduate students prepare to take the GRE Computer Science Test. The book contains the actual GRE Computer Science Test administered in October 1990, along with a section of sample questions, and includes information about the purpose of the GRE Subject Tests, a detailed description of the content specifications for the GRE Computer Science Test, and a description of the procedures for developing the test. All test questions that were scored have been included in the practice test.

The sample questions included in this practice book are organized by content category and represent the types of questions included in the test. The purpose of these questions is to provide some indication of the range of topics covered in the test as well as to provide some additional questions for practice purposes. These questions do not represent either the length of the actual test or the proportion of actual test questions within each of the content categories.

Before you take the full-length test, you may want to answer the sample questions. A suggested time limit is provided to give you a rough idea of how much time you would have to complete the sample questions if you were answering them on an actual timed test. After answering the sample questions, evaluate your performance within content categories to determine whether you would benefit by reviewing certain courses.

This practice book contains a complete test book, including the general instructions printed on the back cover and inside back cover. When you take the test at the test center, you will be given time to read these instructions. They show you how to mark your answer sheet properly and give you advice about guessing.

Try to take this practice test under conditions that simulate those in an actual test administration. Use the answer sheets provided on pages 83 to 86 and mark your answers with a No. 2 (soft-lead) pencil as you will do at the test center. Give yourself 2 hours and 50 minutes in a quiet place and work through the test without interruption, focusing your attention on the questions with the same concentration you would use in taking the test to earn a score. Since you will not be permitted to use them at the test center, do not use keyboards, dictionaries or other books, compasses, pamphlets, protractors, highlighter pens, rulers, slide rules, calculators (including watch calculators), stereos or radios with headphones, watch alarms including those with flashing lights or alarm sounds, or paper of any kind.

After you complete the practice test, use the work sheet and conversion tables on pages 39 and 40 to score your test. The work sheet also shows the estimated percent of GRE Computer Science Test examinees from a recent three-year period who answered each question correctly. This will enable you to compare your performance on the questions with theirs. Evaluating your performance on the actual test questions as well as the sample questions should help you determine whether you would benefit further by reviewing certain courses before taking the test at the test center.

We believe that if you use this practice book as we have suggested, you will be able to approach the testing experience with increased confidence.

ADDITIONAL INFORMATION

If you have any questions about any of the information in this book, please write to:

Graduate Record Examinations
Educational Testing Service
P.O. Box 6000
Princeton, NJ 08541-6000

PURPOSE OF THE GRE SUBJECT TESTS

The GRE Subject Tests are designed to help graduate school admission commit-
tees and fellowship sponsors assess the qualifications of applicants in their
subject fields. The tests also provide students with an assessment of their own
qualifications.

Scores on the tests are intended to indicate students' knowledge of the subject
matter emphasized in many undergraduate programs as preparation for graduate
study. Since past achievement is usually a good indicator of future performance,
the scores are helpful in predicting students' success in graduate study. Because
the tests are standardized, the test scores permit comparison of students from
different institutions with different undergraduate programs.

The Graduate Record Examinations Board recommends that scores on the
Subject Tests be considered in conjunction with other relevant information about
applicants. Because numerous factors influence success in graduate school,
reliance on a single measure to predict success is not advisable. Other indicators
of competence typically include undergraduate transcripts showing courses taken
and grades earned, letters of recommendation, and GRE General Test scores.

DEVELOPMENT OF THE GRE COMPUTER SCIENCE TEST

Each new edition of the Computer Science Test is developed by a committee of
examiners composed of professors in the subject who are on undergraduate and
graduate faculties in different types of institutions and in different regions of the
United States. In selecting members for the committee of examiners, the GRE
Program seeks the advice of the Association for Computing Machinery (ACM)
and the Computer Society of the Institute of Electrical and Electronic Engineers
(IEEE).

The content and scope of each test are specified and reviewed periodically by
the committee of examiners who, along with other faculty members who are also
subject-matter specialists, write the test questions. All questions proposed for the
test are reviewed by the committee and revised as necessary. The accepted
questions are assembled into a test in accordance with the content specifications
developed by the committee of examiners to ensure adequate coverage of the
various aspects of the field and at the same time to prevent overemphasis on any
single topic. The entire test is then reviewed and approved by the committee.

Subject-matter and measurement specialists on the ETS staff assist the
committee of examiners, providing information and advice about methods of
test construction and helping to prepare the questions and assemble the test. In
addition, they review every test question to identify and eliminate language,
symbols, or content considered to be potentially offensive, inappropriate, or
serving to perpetuate any negative attitudes toward individuals or groups of

people. The test as a whole is also reviewed to make sure that the test questions, where applicable, include an appropriate balance of people in different groups and different roles.

Because of the diversity of undergraduate curricula in computer science, it is not possible for a single test to cover all the material an examinee may have studied. The examiners, therefore, select questions that test the basic knowledge and understanding most important for successful graduate study in the field. The committee keeps the test up-to-date by regularly developing new editions and revising existing editions. In this way, the test content changes steadily but gradually, much like most curricula.

When a new edition is introduced into the program, it is equated; that is, the scores are related by statistical methods to scores on previous editions so that scores from all editions in use are directly comparable. Although they do not contain the same questions, all editions of the Computer Science Test are constructed according to equivalent specifications for content and level of difficulty, and all measure equivalent knowledge and skills.

After a new edition of the Computer Science Test is first administered, examinees' responses to each test question are analyzed to determine whether the question functioned as expected. This analysis may reveal that a question is ambiguous, requires knowledge beyond the scope of the test, or is inappropriate for the group or a particular subgroup of examinees taking the test. Such questions are not counted in computing examinees' scores.

CONTENT OF THE GRE COMPUTER SCIENCE TEST

The test consists of about 80 multiple-choice questions, some of which are grouped in sets and based on such materials as diagrams, graphs, and program fragments.

The approximate distribution of questions in each edition of the test according to content categories is indicated by the following outline. The percentages given are approximate; actual percentages will vary slightly from one edition of the test to another.

I. SOFTWARE SYSTEMS AND METHODOLOGY — 35%
   A. Data organization
      1. Data types
      2. Data structures and implementation techniques
      3. File organization (e.g., sequential, indexed, multilevel)
   B. Program control
      1. Iteration and recursion
      2. Functions, procedures, and exception handlers
      3. Communication and synchronization

C. Programming languages and notation
1. Constructs for data organization and program control
2. Scope, binding, and parameter passing
3. Expression evaluation
D. Systems
1. Compilers and interpreters
2. Operating systems, including resource management and protection/security
3. Networking and distributed systems
4. System development tools
5. System performance

II. COMPUTER ORGANIZATION AND ARCHITECTURE — 20%
A. Logic design
1. Implementation of combinational and sequential circuits
2. Functional properties of digital integrated circuits
B. Processors and control units
1. Instruction sets
2. Register and ALU organization
3. Number representation
4. Control sequencing
5. Data paths
C. Memories and their hierarchies
1. Speed, capacity, cost, allocation
2. Cache, main, secondary storage
3. Virtual memory, paging, segmentation
D. Communication
1. Bus, switch, and network structures and protocols
2. I/O
3. Synchronization
E. High-performance architectures
1. Pipelining
2. Multiprocessors
3. Vector processors

III. THEORY — 20%
A. Automata and language theory
1. Models of computation (finite automata, pushdown automata, Turing machines)
2. Formal languages (regular languages, context free languages)
3. Decidability
B. Design and analysis of algorithms and computational complexity
1. Exact or asymptotic analysis of the best, worst, or average case for the time and space complexity of specific algorithms
2. Upper and lower bounds on the complexity of specific problems
3. NP-completeness
C. Correctness of programs
1. Formal specifications and assertions
2. Verification techniques

IV. MATHEMATICAL BACKGROUND — 20%
   A. Discrete structures
      1. Mathematical logic
      2. Elementary combinatorics, including graph theory and counting arguments
      3. Elementary discrete mathematics, including number theory, discrete probability, recurrence relations
   B. Numerical mathematics
      1. Computer arithmetic, including number representations, roundoff, overflow and underflow
      2. Classical numerical algorithms
      3. Linear algebra
V. ADVANCED TOPICS — 5%
   Topics including modeling and simulation, information retrieval, artificial intelligence, computer graphics, data communications, databases, VLSI.

SAMPLE QUESTIONS

The sample questions included in this practice book are organized by content category and represent the types of questions included in the test. The purpose of these questions is to provide some indication of the range of topics covered in the test as well as to provide some additional questions for practice purposes. **These questions do not represent either the length of the actual test or the proportion of actual test questions within each of the content categories.** A time limit of between 135 and 140 minutes is suggested to give you a rough idea of how much time you would have to complete the sample questions if you were answering them on an actual timed test. However, in answering the sample questions, you should realize that they are arranged in increasing order of perceived difficulty **within each of the content categories**, whereas the questions on an actual test are *not* arranged according to content categories, but the whole test has its questions arranged in increasing order of difficulty as perceived by the Committee of Examiners for the test. Correct answers to the sample questions are listed on page 36.

NOTATION AND CONVENTIONS

In the sample questions, a reading knowledge of Pascal-like languages is assumed. The following notational conventions are used.

1. All numbers are assumed to be written in decimal notation unless otherwise indicated.

2. $\lfloor x \rfloor$ denotes the greatest integer that is less than or equal to x .

3. $\lceil x \rceil$ denotes the least integer that is greater than or equal to x .

4. $g(n) = O(f(n))$ denotes "$g(n)$ has order at most $f(n)$" and means that there exist positive constants C and N such that $|g(n)| \leq Cf(n)$ for all $n > N$.

    $g(n) = \Omega(f(n))$ denotes "$g(n)$ has order at least $f(n)$" and for this test means that there exist positive constants C and N such that $g(n) \geq Cf(n)$ for all $n > N$.

    $g(n) = \theta(f(n))$ denotes "$g(n)$ has the same order as $f(n)$" and means that there exist positive constants C_1 , C_2 , and N such that $C_1 f(n) \leq g(n) \leq C_2 f(n)$ for all $n > N$.

5. $\exists$ denotes "there exists."

    $\forall$ denotes "for all."

    $\Rightarrow$ denotes "implies."

    $\neg$ denotes "not"; "$\bar{A}$" is also used as meaning "$\neg A$."

    $\vee$ denotes "inclusive or"; + also denotes "inclusive or."

    $\oplus$ denotes "exclusive or."

    $\wedge$ denotes "and"; also, juxtaposition of statements denotes "and," e.g., PQ denotes "P and Q."

    $\emptyset$ denotes the empty set.

6. If A and B denote sets, then:

    $A \cup B$ is the set of all elements that are in A or in B or in both;

    $A \cap B$ is the set of all elements that are in both A and B ; AB also denotes $A \cap B$;

    $\bar{A}$ is the set of all elements not in A that are in some specified universal set.

7. In a string expression, if S and T denote strings or sets of strings, then:

    An empty string is denoted by ϵ or by Λ ;

    ST denotes the concatenation of S and T ;

    $S + T$ denotes $S \cup T$ or $\{S, T\}$, depending on context;

    S^n denotes $\underbrace{SS \ldots S}_{n \text{ factors}}$;

    S^* denotes $\epsilon + S + S^2 + S^3 + \ldots$;

    S^+ denotes $S + S^2 + S^3 + \ldots$.

GO ON TO THE NEXT PAGE.

8. In a grammar:

    $\alpha \rightarrow \beta$ represents a production in the grammar.

    $\alpha \Rightarrow \beta$ means β can be derived from α by the application of exactly one production.

    $\alpha \overset{*}{\Rightarrow} \beta$ means β can be derived from α by the application of zero or more productions.

    Unless otherwise specified

    (i)   symbols appearing on the left-hand side of productions are nonterminal symbols, the remaining symbols are terminal symbols,

    (ii) the leftmost symbol of the first production is the start symbol, and

    (iii) the start symbol is permitted to appear on the right-hand side of productions.

9. In a logic diagram:

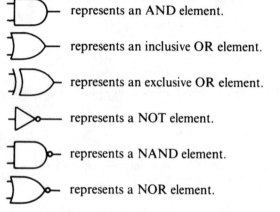

    represents an AND element.

    represents an inclusive OR element.

    represents an exclusive OR element.

    represents a NOT element.

    represents a NAND element.

    represents a NOR element.

10. input — $\boxed{\begin{array}{c} D \quad Q \\ \triangleright \quad \overline{Q} \end{array}}$ — represents a D-type flip-flop, which stores the value of its D input when clocked.
    clock —

11. Binary tree traversal is defined recursively as follows:

    preorder - visit the root, traverse the left subtree, traverse the right subtree

    inorder   - traverse the left subtree, visit the root, traverse the right subtree

    postorder - traverse the left subtree, traverse the right subtree, visit the root

12. In a finite automaton diagram, states are represented by circles, with final (or accepting) states indicated by two concentric circles. The start state is indicated by the word "Start." An arc from state s to state t labeled a indicates a transition from s to t on input a. A label a/b indicates that this transition produces an output b. A label $a_1, a_2, \ldots, a_k$ indicates that the transition is made on any of the inputs $a_1, a_2, \ldots, a_k$.

GO ON TO THE NEXT PAGE.

I. SOFTWARE SYSTEMS AND METHODOLOGY

1. With regard to the Pascal declarations

    type

        Vector = **array**[1..10] **of** *integer* ;

    var

        a   : *Vector* ;

        b,c : **array**[1..10] **of** *integer* ;

        d   : *Vector* ;

    which of the following is FALSE ?

    (A) *a* and *b* have structurally equivalent types.
    (B) *a* and *d* have name equivalent types.
    (C) *b* and *c* have structurally equivalent types.
    (D) *b* and *d* have name equivalent types.
    (E) *a*, *c*, and *d* have structurally equivalent types.

2. In the NoNicks operating system, the time required by a single file-read operation has four <u>nonoverlapping</u> components:

    > disk seek time—25 msec
    > disk latency time—8 msec
    > disk transfer time—1 msec per 1,000 bytes
    > operating system overhead—1 msec per 1,000 bytes + 10 msec

    In version 1 of the system, the file read retrieved blocks of 1,000 bytes. In version 2, the file read (along with the underlying layout on disk) was modified to retrieve blocks of 4,000 bytes. The ratio of the time required to read a large file under version 2 to the time required to read the same large file under version 1 is approximately

    (A) 1:4   (B) 1:3.5   (C) 1:1   (D) 1.1:1   (E) 2.7:1

3. Sometimes the object module produced by a compiler includes information (from the symbol table) mapping all source program names to their addresses. The most likely purpose of this information is

    (A) for use as input to a debugging aid
    (B) to increase the run-time efficiency of the program
    (C) for the reduction of the symbol-table space needed by the compiler
    (D) to tell the loader where each variable belongs
    (E) to tell the operating system what to call the variables

Questions 4-5 are based on the following program fragment written in a Pascal-like language.

L1 : **begin**

   var *a, b, c* : *integer* ;   (1)

   var *d, e* : *real* ;

   _____
   _____
   _____

L2 : **begin**

   var *a, f* : *integer* ;

   var *g, h* : *real* ;

   _____
   _____
   _____

   end ;

   end

Let the designation "block *Li*" refer to all the statements from the **begin** labeled with *Li* to its corresponding **end**.

4. In block *L2* the variables *g* and *h* are best described as

(A) dummy variables   (B) parameter variables   (C) global variables

(D) local variables   (E) recursive variables

5. If the notation *L1-L2* means "the portion of block *L1* that is not in block *L2*," then the scopes of the variables *a* and *b* declared in the statement numbered (1) are

(A) *L1* for *a* and *L1* for *b*   (B) *L1* for *a* and *L1-L2* for *b*   (C) *L1-L2* for *a* and *L1* for *b*

(D) *L1-L2* for *a* and *L1-L2* for *b*   (E) *L2* for *a* and *L2* for *b*

6. Suppose there is an open (external) hash table with four buckets, numbered 0,1,2,3, and integers are hashed into these buckets using hash function $h(x) = x \bmod 4$. If the sequence of perfect squares $1,4,9, \ldots, i^2, \ldots$ is hashed into the table, then, as the total number of entries in the table grows, what will happen?

(A) Two of the buckets will each get approximately half the entries, and the other two will remain empty.
(B) All buckets will receive approximately the same number of entries.
(C) All entries will go into one particular bucket.
(D) All buckets will receive entries, but the difference between the buckets with smallest and largest number of entries will grow.
(E) Three of the buckets will each get approximately one-third of the entries, and the fourth bucket will remain empty.

7. Two single-user workstations are attached to the same local area network. On one of these workstations, file pages are accessed over the network from a file server; the average access time per page is 0.1 second. On the other of these workstations, file pages are accessed from a local disk; the average access time per page is 0.05 second.

A particular compilation requires 30 seconds of computation and 200 file page accesses. What is the ratio of the total time required by this compilation if run on the diskless (file server) workstation to the total time required if run on the workstation with the local disk, if it is assumed that computation is not overlapped with file access?

(A) 1/1   (B) 5/4   (C) 5/3   (D) 10/5   (E) 3/1

8. Two expressions E and F are said to be <u>unifiable</u> if there are substitutions for the variables of E and F that make the expressions lexically identical. In the following three expressions, only w, x, y, and z are variables.

    I. $f(w,w)$
   II. $f(x,1)$
  III. $f(y,g(z))$

Which pairs of these expressions is(are) pairs of unifiable expressions?

(A) (I, II) only
(B) (I, III) only
(C) (II, III) only
(D) (I, II) and (I, III) only
(E) (I, II), (I, III), and (II, III)

9. Several concurrent processes are attempting to share an I/0 device. In an attempt to achieve mutual exclusion, each process is given the following structure. (*Busy* is a shared Boolean variable.)

    < code unrelated to device use >

    repeat
    until *Busy* = *false* ;

    Busy := *true* ;

    < code to access shared device >

    Busy := *false* ;

    < code unrelated to device use >

Which of the following is(are) true of this approach?

    I. It provides a reasonable solution to the problem of guaranteeing mutual exclusion.
   II. It may consume substantial CPU time accessing the *Busy* variable.
  III. It will fail to guarantee mutual exclusion.

(A) I only   (B) II only   (C) III only   (D) I and II   (E) II and III

15

10. The construct

> **cobegin** *Statement1* ; *Statement2* **coend**

means *Statement1* and *Statement2* are to be executed in parallel. The only two atomic actions in this construct are loading the value of a variable and storing into a variable. For the program segment

```
x := 0 ;
y := 0 ;
cobegin
  begin
    x := 1 ;
    y := y + x
  end ;
  begin
    y := 2 ;
    x := x + 3
  end
coend
```

which of the following indicate(s) possible values for the variables when the segment finishes execution?

   I. $x = 1$, $y = 2$

  II. $x = 1$, $y = 3$

 III. $x = 4$, $y = 6$

(A) I only
(B) I and II only
(C) I and III only
(D) II and III only
(E) I, II, and III

11. The following algorithm solves a system of equations $Lx = b$ where L is a unit lower-triangular matrix (ones on the diagonal and zeros above the diagonal).

```
for i := 1 to n do
  x[i] := b[i] ;
for i := 2 to n do
  for j := 1 to i - 1 do
    < statement >
```

The missing $<$ statement $>$ in the algorithm above is

(A) $x[i] := x[i] - L[i,j]*x[j]$

(B) $x[j] := x[j] - L[i,j]*x[i]$

(C) $x[j] := x[j] - L[i,j]*x[j]$

(D) $x[i] := b[j] - L[i,j]*x[i]$

(E) $x[i] := x[i] - L[i,j]*x[i]$

12. A lexical analyzer for Pascal scans the input character-by-character, from a beginning point p until it knows what token begins at p. Assume that the tokens of Pascal are the usual ones: identifiers, constants, keywords, and operators. Sometimes the lexical analyzer must scan beyond the token that begins at p in order to determine what that token is. For which of the following character strings can a lexical analyzer for Pascal determine, without looking at the next character, that it has seen the complete token?

    I.   then
   II.   <
  III.   ;

(A) None   (B) I only   (C) III only   (D) I and II   (E) II and III

13. The following syntax-directed translation scheme is used with a shift-reduce (bottom-up) parser that performs the action in braces immediately after any reduction by the corresponding production.

    $A \rightarrow aB$ {print "0"}
    $A \rightarrow c$ {print "1"}
    $B \rightarrow Ab$ {print "2"}

The string printed when the parser input is aacbb is

(A) 00122   (B) 02021   (C) 10202   (D) 12020   (E) 22100

14. For procedures $P1$, $P2$, $P3$, and for Boolean variable B, the repeat loop

    $P1$;
    repeat
      $P2$
    until B ;
    $P3$

is sometimes incorrectly transformed to

    (i) $P1$;
   (ii) **while not** B **do**
  (iii) $P2$;
  (iv) $P3$

The correct version of this transformation is obtained from the incorrect result above by

(A) replacing "**not** B" with "B" in line (ii)
(B) moving line (i) to between lines (ii) and (iii)
(C) adding a copy of line (iii) between lines (i) and (ii)
(D) adding a copy of line (iv) between lines (ii) and (iii)
(E) replacing "$P1$" by "**if** B **then** $P1$"

15. A stack can be defined abstractly by the following rules. Let s be a stack, and let X be a symbol. Then:

     (1) ϵ, the "empty stack," is a stack.

     (2) $PUSH(s, X)$ is a stack.

     (3) $POP(PUSH(s, X)) = s$

     (4) $TOP(PUSH(s, X)) = X$

For example:

$$TOP(POP(PUSH(PUSH(\epsilon, X), Y)))$$
$$= TOP(PUSH(\epsilon, X)) \quad \text{[rule 3 with } s = PUSH(\epsilon, X)]$$
$$= X \quad \text{[rule 4 with } s = \epsilon]$$

All of the following are derivable from statements (1), (2), (3), and (4) EXCEPT:

(A) $TOP(PUSH(PUSH(\epsilon, X), Y)) = Y$

(B) $POP(PUSH(\epsilon, X)) = \epsilon$

(C) $PUSH(POP(PUSH(\epsilon, X)), Y)$ is a stack.

(D) $TOP(PUSH(POP(PUSH(\epsilon, X)), Y)) = Y$

(E) $POP(POP(PUSH(\epsilon, X))) = X$

16. For $x \geqq 0$, $y \geqq 0$, define $A(x, y)$ by

$$A(0, y) = y + 1,$$
$$A(x + 1, 0) = A(x, 1), \text{ and}$$
$$A(x + 1, y + 1) = A(x, A(x + 1, y)).$$

Then, for all non-negative integers y, $A(1, y)$ is

(A) 2

(B) $y + 1$

(C) $y + 2$

(D) $2y + 3$

(E) none of the above

17. The following program is written in a language having the syntax of Pascal, but one in which passing parameters might not be limited to call by value and call by reference, as in Pascal.

```
program Param(input,output) ;
var
  a,b : integer ;
  procedure p(x,y : integer) ;
  begin
    x := x+2 ;
    a := x*y ;
    x := x+1
  end ;
begin
  a := 1 ;
  b := 2 ;
  p(a,b) ;
  writeln(a)
end.
```

Under which of the following parameter-passing mechanisms will the output of the program be 4 ?

(A) Call by value
(B) Call by reference
(C) Call by name
(D) Call by value-result
(E) None of the above

18. Consider the following algorithm for $n > 0$.

```
const
    n = < some positive integer > ;

var
    a,b,p,Sum : integer ;

begin
    a := 0;   b := n;   Sum := 0 ;
    readln(p) ;
    while  a < n  and  b > 0  do
      begin
        if  p > 0  then
          begin
            a := a + 1 ;
            Sum := Sum + 1
          end
        else
          begin
            a := a - 1 ;
            b := b - 1 ;
            Sum := Sum + 1
          end ;
        Modify(p)  { p is called by reference, and Modify }
                   { does not affect the value of any     }
                   { other variable.                      }
      end
end
```

Of the following, which best approximates the largest possible value of *Sum* when the algorithm terminates?

(A) $3n$
(B) $4n$
(C) $5n$
(D) $2n^2$
(E) $3n^2$

19. A microcomputer used for data acquisition and control is required to digitize and process four analog input signals and to output their average continually; i.e., in real time. The time for an external analog-to-digital converter (which is triggered by a CPU instruction) to digitize one input is 12 microseconds, and only one digitization occurs at a time. Five CPU instructions, including the triggering instruction, must be executed for each signal digitized. Ten CPU instructions are executed in order to average each set of four samples and output this value. The time to convert the output from digital to analog form is to be ignored. If it is assumed that suitable data buffering is employed, then the maximum average instruction execution time that allows the microcomputer to keep up with the input-output data rates, is

(A) 0.8 μs   (B) 1.2 μs   (C) 1.6 μs   (D) 2.4 μs   (E) 3.2 μs

20. Two alternatives for interconnecting a set of processors with bidirectional links are (1) the fully interconnected network, in which each processor is directly connected to every other processor, and (2) the ring network, in which each processor is connected to two other processors. The worst-case path length for a network is the maximum, over all pairs of nodes in the network, of the minimum length paths (measured in number of links) between the nodes. For each type of interconnection of n processors, a figure of merit can be formed as the product of the number of links required for the network times the worst-case path length connecting any two processors. The ratio of this figure of merit for the fully interconnected network compared to that of the ring network, for even $n > 2$, is

(A) $1/(n^2)$ (B) $1/(n(n-1))$ (C) $1/n$ (D) $(n-1)/n$ (E) $(n-1)/(2n)$

20

Questions 21-22 are based on a complex assembly line of four stages designed with feedback so that a given item can go through a single state more than once. Two or more stages can act on the item during one time unit. This assembly line is described by the table below, in which an X in row S_i and column t_j indicates that at time t_j, stage S_i is acting on the item that entered the assembly line at time t_0.

	t_0	t_1	t_2	t_3	t_4	t_5	t_6
S_0	X					X	
S_1			X				X
S_2		X		X			
S_3			X		X		

21. If each stage can act on only one item in any time unit, at which time unit(s) between t_1 and t_6 could one introduce a second item into this assembly line?

(A) t_1 only   (B) t_1 or t_3 only   (C) t_1 or t_4 only

(D) t_1 or t_3 or t_6 only   (E) t_1 or t_3 or t_4 or t_6

22. If throughput is to be maximized for the assembly line, at which constant interval, measured in time units, could new items be periodically introduced without violating the time constraints?

(A) 1   (B) 2   (C) 3   (D) 6   (E) 7

Questions 23-24 are based on the table below, which lists eight jobs to be scheduled on two identical processors, the times at which these jobs become available, and their required processing times. Assume that jobs can be scheduled instantly.

Job	Available	Processing Time
A	0	6
B	0	2
C	0	3
D	2	5
E	3	4
F	5	1
G	7	3
H	9	6

23. What is the earliest time at which processing of all jobs can be completed?

(A) 14   (B) 15   (C) 16   (D) 17   (E) 18

24. For the preceding table, assume that the criterion for scheduling is to minimize the delay in starting the processing of each job and assume no preemption. This minimum average delay in starting time is most nearly

(A) 1   (B) 1.25   (C) 1.38   (D) 1.5   (E) 1.75

II. COMPUTER ORGANIZATION AND ARCHITECTURE

25. A major advantage of direct mapping of a cache is its simplicity. The main disadvantage of this organization is that

    (A) it does not allow simultaneous access to the intended data and its tag
    (B) it is more expensive than other types of cache organizations
    (C) the cache hit ratio is degraded if two or more blocks used alternately map onto the same block frame in the cache
    (D) its access time is greater than that of other cache organizations
    (E) the number of blocks required for the cache increases linearly with the size of the main memory

26. Two computers communicate with each other by sending data packets across a local area network. The size of these packets is 1,000 bytes. The network has the capacity to carry 1,000 packets per second. The CPU time required to execute the network protocol to send one packet is 10 milliseconds. The maximum rate at which one computer can send data to another is approximately

    (A)   10,000 bytes/second
    (B)   25,000 bytes/second
    (C)   100,000 bytes/second
    (D)   500,000 bytes/second
    (E)   1,000,000 bytes/second

27.

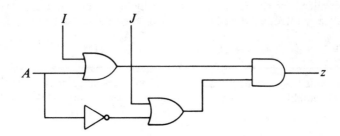

The circuit above is to be used to implement the function $z = f(A,B) = \overline{A} + B$. Inputs I and J can be selected from the set $\{0, 1, B, \overline{B}\}$. What values should be chosen for I and J?

(A) $I = 0, J = B$ (B) $I = 1, J = B$ (C) $I = B, J = 1$ (D) $I = \overline{B}, J = 0$ (E) $I = 1, J = \overline{B}$

22

Questions 28-29 are concerned with a single-surface disk drive having the following characteristics.

Number of tracks per disk:	35
Number of sectors per track:	10
Bits per second transfer rate:	250,000
Revolutions per minute rotational speed:	300

Assume that one byte is 8 bits.

28. If no gaps or special formatting is assumed, then the nominal storage capacity, in bytes, of one such disk is

(A) 6,250   (B) 29,267   (C) 218,750   (D) 1,750,000

(E) none of the above

29. Assume that data transfers between the disk and the memory of a host system are interrupt-driven, one byte at a time. If the instructions to accomplish a one-byte transfer take $8\,\mu s$ and the interrupt overhead is $10\,\mu s$, then the time available, in μs, for other computing between byte transfers is

(A) 0   (B) 8   (C) 10   (D) 14   (E) 32

Questions 30-31 are based on the following information.

In the microprogrammed control unit of the Cucumber-XMP computer, the output of the control store is loaded into a control register. The control store may be addressed from any of three sources: (i) the output of a micro-program counter for sequential access of microinstructions; (ii) a field in the control register to effect a branch microinstruction; (iii) an additional input to which are connected signals derived from other parts of the Cucumber.

30. The additional input is LEAST likely to be used for signals derived from the

(A) CPU instruction opcode
(B) CPU instruction address
(C) CPU instruction addressing mode bits
(D) arithmetic logic unit condition codes
(E) interrupts and/or other types of exception

31. Suppose that the same clock signal is used to increment the microprogram counter and to load the control register. Which of the following assertions is (are) true?
    I.   Microinstruction execution time is at least two clock periods.
    II. Microinstruction execution can be overlapped with fetching the next microinstruction.
    III. Unconditional branch microinstructions must necessarily take longer than other types.

(A) I only   (B) II only   (C) III only   (D) I and III   (E) II and III

---

32. A 10-unit heap of memory uses an allocation algorithm in which a block is allocated at the left end of the leftmost block in which it fits. Which of the following allocation/deallocation patterns CANNOT be satisfied?

(A) $x := alloc(10)$; $free(x)$; $y := alloc(3)$
(B) $x := alloc(5)$; $y := alloc(3)$; $free(x)$; $z := alloc(6)$
(C) $x := alloc(1)$; $free(x)$; $x := alloc(6)$; $y := alloc(4)$
(D) $x := alloc(9)$; $y := alloc(1)$; $free(x)$; $z := alloc(8)$; $w := alloc(1)$
(E) $x := alloc(5)$; $y := alloc(1)$; $free(x)$; $z := alloc(3)$; $w := alloc(4)$; $v := alloc(2)$

33. The figure below shows a control circuit, consisting of a 3-bit register and some combinational logic. This circuit is initially in the state $Q_1 Q_2 Q_3 = 000$. On subsequent clock pulses, the circuit is required to generate the control sequence: $(100) \rightarrow (010) \rightarrow (001) \rightarrow (001) \rightarrow (001) \rightarrow \ldots$

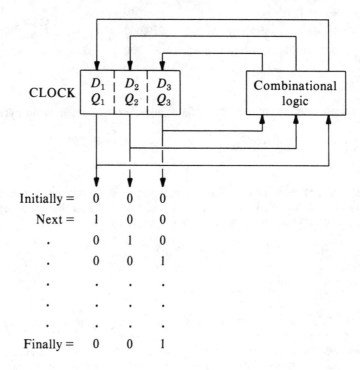

Initially =	0	0	0
Next =	1	0	0
.	0	1	0
.	0	0	1
.	.	.	.
.	.	.	.
.	.	.	.
Finally =	0	0	1

Which of the following is a correct set of equations to be implemented by the combinational logic?

(A) $D_1 = \bar{Q}_1 \bar{Q}_2 \bar{Q}_3$, $D_2 = Q_1$, $D_3 = Q_2 \vee Q_3$

(B) $D_1 = \bar{Q}_1 \bar{Q}_2 \bar{Q}_3$, $D_2 = Q_1 \bar{Q}_2 \bar{Q}_3$, $D_3 = \bar{Q}_1 Q_2 \bar{Q}_3$

(C) $D_1 = \bar{Q}_1$, $D_2 = \bar{Q}_2$, $D_3 = \bar{Q}_3$

(D) $D_1 = \bar{Q}_1 \bar{Q}_2$, $D_2 = \bar{Q}_2 \bar{Q}_3$, $D_3 = \bar{Q}_3 \bar{Q}_1$

(E) $D_1 = Q_3$, $D_2 = Q_1$, $D_3 = Q_2$

34.

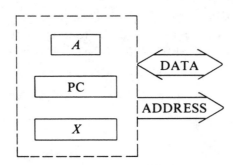

A hypothetical microprocessor communicates with its memory and peripherals over an 8-bit data bus and a 16-bit address bus. It contains an 8-bit accumulator A and two 16-bit registers: program counter PC and index register X. (see diagram above.) The opcode of each instruction is one byte (8 bits) long. Assume that any internal processor time is negligible and that the time to address memory and transfer one byte in either direction over the data bus equals unity (one memory cycle).

The time taken to fetch and execute the 3-byte instruction "store A in some address indexed by X" is

(A) 3   (B) 4   (C) 5   (D) 6   (E) 7

35.

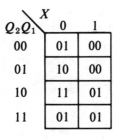

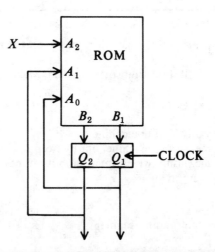

The state table for a controller with a single input X is shown on the left above. It is to be implemented by means of an 8-word by 2-bit, read-only memory (ROM) and a 2-bit register, as shown on the right above. A_2 is the most significant address bit of the ROM. (When X changes, it does so synchronously with the CLOCK, so that it does not cause a race condition.) Which of the following lists the requisite contents of ROM locations 0-7, respectively?

(A) 10 00 10 00 11 01 01 01

(B) 01 10 11 01 00 00 01 01

(C) 01 10 01 11 00 00 01 01

(D) 01 00 10 00 01 01 11 01

(E) 01 00 00 10 11 01 01 01

36. Sam and Sue are using a program P to generate personalized greeting cards on their Cucumber AT micro-computer. Business is so good that they must generate one card every 3 seconds. However, the memory requirements of a run of program P range between 0 and 1,000,000 bytes, distributed uniformly. Furthermore, if a run requires r bytes, and the Cucumber's memory is m bytes, then the run takes

   (i)   1 second if $r \leqq m$, and takes

   (ii) r/m seconds if $r > m$, because of byte swapping.

The minimum amount of memory that Sam and Sue must buy so that they can produce an average of one card every 3 seconds is approximately

(A) 172,000 bytes   (B) 333,000 bytes   (C) 484,000 bytes

(D) 732,000 bytes   (E) 889,000 bytes

37. Which of the following sorting algorithms has average-case and worst-case running times of $O(n \log n)$?

    (A) Bubble sort   (B) Insertion sort   (C) Merge sort   (D) Quicksort   (E) Selection sort

38. The language $\{ww \,|\, w \in (0 + 1)^*\}$ is

    (A) not accepted by any Turing machine
    (B) accepted by some Turing machine, but by no pushdown automaton
    (C) accepted by some pushdown automaton, but not context-free
    (D) context-free, but not regular
    (E) regular

39. Consider the following program fragment.

    (1)   **for** $i := 1$ **to** n **do**
    (2) $M[i] := 0$

    Let A represent the initialization ($i := 1$) in line (1) ; let B represent the "body" of the loop; i.e., line (2). Let I represent the incrementation of i by 1 implied by line (1), and let T represent the test for $i \leq n$ also implied by line (1).

    Which of the following regular expressions represents all possible sequences of steps taken during execution of the fragment, if it is assumed that n is arbitrary and that no abnormal terminations of the loop can occur?

    (A) $AT(BIT)^*$ (B) $A(ITB)^*T$ (C) $AT^*B^*I^*T$ (D) $(ABIT)^*$ (E) $A(TBI)^*$

40.

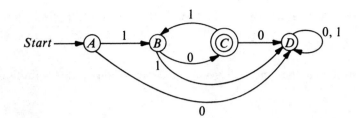

In the figure above, a finite automaton M has start state A and accepting state C. Which of the following regular expressions denotes the set of words accepted by M?

(A) 10^* (B) $(10)^*$ (C) 10^*1^*0 (D) $1(01)^*0$ (E) $(01)^*01$

41. Which of the regular expressions below describes the same set of strings as the following grammar (with root S)?

$$S \longrightarrow Ax \mid By$$
$$A \longrightarrow y \mid Ay$$
$$B \longrightarrow x \mid y$$

(A) $y^*x + xy + y$ (B) $y^*x + x + yy$ (C) $yy^*x + xy + y$

(D) $y^*x + xy + yy$ (E) $yy^*x + xy + yy$

42. Consider the following program segment for finding the minimum value of an array.

```
var
    i,j : integer ;
    a : array[1..N] of real ;
begin
    j := 1 ;
    for i := 2 to N do
        if a[i] < a[j] then
            j := i
end
```

Which of the following conditions is (are) true each time the condition of the **if-then** statement is tested?

   I. $2 \leq i \leq N$

  II. $a[j] \leq a[k]$ for all k such that $1 \leq k < i$.

 III. $a[j] \leq a[k]$ for all k such that $2 \leq k \leq i$.

(A) I only   (B) II only   (C) I and II only   (D) I and III only   (E) I, II, and III

27

43. Let the syntactic category $<S>$ be defined by the Backus-Naur form description:

$$<S> ::= r\, \ell\, |\, r <S> \ell\, |\, <S><S>$$

Which of the following strings can be generated from $<S>$ according to this definition?

   I.   rr ℓ ℓ r ℓ

   II. r ℓ ℓ r r r ℓ ℓ

   III. rr ℓ r ℓ r ℓ ℓ r ℓ rr ℓ

(A) I only   (B) II only   (C) III only   (D) I and III   (E) II and III

44. Consider N employee records to be stored in memory for on-line retrieval. Each employee record is uniquely identified by a social security number. Consider the following ways to store the N records.

   I.   An array sorted by social security number
   II.   A linked list sorted by social security number
   III. A linked list not sorted
   IV. A balanced binary search tree with social security number as key

For the structures I-IV, respectively, the average time for an efficient program to find an employee record, given the social security number as key, is which of the following?

	I	II	III	IV
(A)	$O(\log N)$	$O(N)$	$O(N)$	$O(\log N)$
(B)	$O(N)$	$O(\log N)$	$O(N)$	$O(N)$
(C)	$O(\log N)$	$O(\log N)$	$O(N)$	$O(1)$
(D)	$O(N)$	$O(N)$	$O(N)$	$O(1)$
(E)	$O(N)$	$O(\log N)$	$O(\log N)$	$O(1)$

45. In a height-balanced binary search tree, the heights of the left and right descendents of any node differ by at most 1. Which of the following are true of such a tree?

   I.   Worst-case search time is logarithmic in the number of nodes.
   II.   Average-case search time is logarithmic in the number of nodes.
   III. Best-case search time is proportional to the height of the tree.
   IV. The height of the tree is logarithmic in the number of nodes.

(A) I and III only   (B) II and III only   (C) II and IV only

(D) I, II, and IV   (E) I, III, and IV

46. Three common operations on the symbol table of a compiler are:

> *Insert* — insert an identifier and its attributes
>
> *Find* — return the attributes of a particular identifier
>
> *List*   — list all identifiers and their attributes in lexicographic order

A particular compiler maintains its symbol table as a hash table with $2n$ buckets. For a symbol table with approximately n identifiers, which of the following gives the order of the average cost of efficient programs performing these three operations?

	Insert	*Find*	*List*
(A)	$O(n)$	$O(n)$	$O(n)$
(B)	$O(\log n)$	$O(n)$	$O(n \log n)$
(C)	$O(\log n)$	$O(\log n)$	$O(n)$
(D)	$O(1)$	$O(\log n)$	$O(n)$
(E)	$O(1)$	$O(1)$	$O(n \log n)$

47. If L is a language accepted by some automaton M, which of the following is(are) true?

   I. If M is a nondeterministic finite automaton, then L is accepted by some deterministic finite automaton.
   II. If M is a deterministic pushdown automaton, then L is accepted by some nondeterministic pushdown automaton.
   III. If M is a nondeterministic pushdown automaton, then L is accepted by some deterministic Turing machine.

   (A) I only   (B) III only   (C) I and II only   (D) II and III only   (E) I, II, and III

48. Which of the following assertions has the property that if the assertion is true before executing the program fragment

$$z:=z * a;\ y:=y - 1$$

then it will also be true afterward?

   (A) $a * y = z$ (B) $z = a^y$ (C) $a^b = z * a^y$ (D) $y > 0 \wedge z = a^k$

   (E) None of the above

49. Which of the following regular expressions is equivalent to (describes the same set of strings as) $(a^* + b)^*(c + d)$?

   (A) $a^*(c + d) + b(c + d)$ (B) $a^*(c + d)^* + b(c + d)^*$ (C) $a^*(c + d) + b^*(c + d)$

   (D) $(a + b)^*c + (a + b)^*d$ (E) $(a^* + b)c + (a^* + b)d$

50. The number of 1's in the binary representation of

$$13 \cdot 16^3 + 11 \cdot 16^2 + 9 \cdot 16 + 3$$

is which of the following?

(A) 7   (B) 8   (C) 9   (D) 10   (E) 12

51. The binary relation on the integers defined by

$$R = \{(x, y) : |y - x| \leqq 1\}$$

has which of the following properties?

   I. Reflexivity
  II. Symmetry
 III. Transitivity

(A) None   (B) I and II only   (C) I and III only   (D) II and III only   (E) I, II, and III

52. Consider the part of the two-dimensional integer grid bounded by point $A = (0, 0)$ at the "southwest" corner and by point $B = (n, n)$ at the "northeast" corner. How many different ways are there of walking from A to B on grid lines, always moving between any two grid points either east or north?

(A) 2^{2n} (B) $\binom{2n}{n}$ (C) $n!$ (D) n^2 (E) $n(n+1)/2$

53. A 0-2 binary tree is a rooted tree such that every node has either no child or two children. The height of a binary tree is the maximum number of edges on a path from the root to a leaf. Let $n(h)$ be the minimum number of nodes in a 0-2 binary tree of height h, and let $N(h)$ be the maximum number. For all $h > 0, (n(h), N(h)) =$

(A) $(h + 1, 2^h - 1)$ (B) $(h + 1, 2^{h+1})$ (C) $(h + 1, 2^{h+1} - 1)$

(D) $(2h + 1, 2^h - 1)$ (E) $(2h + 1, 2^{h+1} - 1)$

54. Let A be an $n \times n$ matrix and let P be an $n \times n$ permutation matrix. Which of the following must be true?

(A) $A = P^{-1}AP$ (B) $PA = P(P^{-1}AP)$ (C) $PAP^{-1} = P(P^{-1}AP)P^{-1}$

(D) $AP = (P^{-1}AP)P$ (E) $\det(A) = \det(P^{-1}AP)$

55. Consider a floating-point number system used by a modern computer for solving large numerical problems. Let $\oplus$ denote the floating-point addition in this system. Which of the following statements is true about this system?

(A) If x and y are real numbers with floating-point representations x' and y', respectively, then $x' \oplus y'$ is always the floating-point representation of $x + y$.

(B) The associative law is valid for $\oplus$; i.e.,

$$(u \oplus v) \oplus w = u \oplus (v \oplus w).$$

(C) There are only finitely many floating-point numbers.

(D) The floating-point numbers are equally spaced throughout their range.

(E) None of the above

56. Consider the representation of six-bit numbers by two's complement, one's complement, or by sign and magnitude. In which representation is there overflow from the addition of the integers 011000 and 011000 ?

   (A) Two's complement only
   (B) Sign and magnitude and one's complement only
   (C) Two's complement and one's complement only
   (D) Two's complement and sign and magnitude only
   (E) All three representations

57.

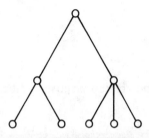

A 2-3 tree is a tree in which

   (i) every interior node has two or three children, and
   (ii) all paths from the root to a leaf have the same length.

An example of a 2-3 tree is shown above. Which of the following could be the number of interior nodes of a 2-3 tree with 9 leaves?

   (A) 5   (B) 6   (C) 7   (D) 8   (E) 9

58. As $n \to \infty$, the function $2^{\sqrt{n}}$ grows faster than

   (A) $\log n$, but slower than $\sqrt{n}$
   (B) $\sqrt{n}$, but slower than n
   (C) n, but slower than n^2
   (D) n^2, but slower than $\sqrt{2^n}$
   (E) $\sqrt{2^n}$, but slower than 2^n

31

59. The bits in the 32-bit word of a hypothetical computer are denoted by:

$$b_{31}b_{30} \ldots b_1 b_0$$

When such a word represents a nonzero floating-point number, its value is taken to be

$$\left(\frac{1}{2} - b_{31}\right)\left(1 + \sum_{i=0}^{23} 2^{i-24} b_i\right) 2^s$$

where $s = -64 + \sum_{i=24}^{30} 2^{i-24} b_i$.

The correct values for the least positive and greatest positive numbers, respectively, that can be represented are given by which of the following pairs?

(A) $2^{-63}, (1 - 2^{-25})2^{64}$

(B) $2^{-64}, (1 - 2^{-24})2^{63}$

(C) $2^{-64}, 2^{63} - 1$

(D) $2^{-65}, (1 - 2^{-25})2^{63}$

(E) $2^{-65}, 2^{64} - 1$

60. Let L_n be the set of integer points (i,j) in the plane satisfying

   i, j integer,
   $i \geqq 0$,
   $j \geqq 0$,
   $i+j \leqq n$.

L_3 is shown below.

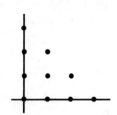

The neighborhood $N_n(i,j)$ of point (i,j) in L_n is all those points (k,m) whose coordinates differ, respectively, from those of (i,j) by at most 1; i.e., $N_n(i,j) = \{ (k,m) \in L_n : \ |i-k| \leqq 1 \ \text{and} \ |j-m| \leqq 1\}$. For different (i,j) in L_n, $N_n(i,j)$ may have different sizes. For $n > 3$, the number of different values that can be the size of $N_n(i,j)$ for some $(i,j) \in L_n$ is

(A) 4   (B) 5   (C) 6   (D) 7   (E) 8

61. Let $b_q b_{q-1} \ldots b_0$ be the binary representation of integer b. The integer 3 is a divisor of b if and only if

(A) $b_1 = b_0 = 1$
(B) the sum of the binary digits b_i is divisible by 9
(C) the sum of the binary digits b_i is divisible by 3 but not by 9
(D) the alternating sum $b_0 - b_1 + b_2 - \ldots$ is zero
(E) the alternating sum $b_0 - b_1 + b_2 - \ldots$ is divisible by 3

Questions 62-63 are based on the following information.

A monochrome bitmap display treats the screen as a rectangular array of pixels (small dots). One bit of memory is associated with each pixel. A pixel is displayed in black if the associated bit is 1, white if it is 0.

The basic operation on such a display causes each bit in a rectangle, *Destination*, to be replaced by the result obtained by applying a Boolean operation to this bit and the corresponding bit in another rectangle, *Source*. (Assume that *Source* and *Destination* are of identical dimensions and nonoverlapping.) There are 16 possible operations corresponding to the 16 possible truth tables of the form:

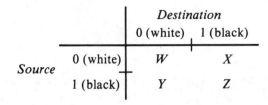

For example, *X* is the Boolean value that will be assigned to any bit in *Destination* that has an original value of 1 and that has a corresponding bit in *Source* whose value is 0. Let *Source* and *Destination* be as follows.

Source	Destination

62. The operation $W=0$ $X=1$ applied to *Source* and *Destination* would yield which of the

$Y=1$ $Z=1$

following results?

(A) (B) (C) 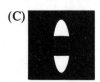 (D) 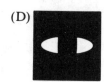 (E)

63. What set of values

   W   *X*

   Y   *Z*

would yield the result

when applied to *Source* and *Destination* as given?

(A) 0 0	(B) 1 0	(C) 1 1	(D) 1 1	(E) 0 1
0 1	0 1	0 0	0 1	0 0

---

64. An information-retrieval system stores records with 5-bit keys. In response to a given query, which is a 5-bit key q, the system lists all records whose keys k have Hamming distance at most 1 from q; i.e., k and q differ in at most one bit position. Suppose the keys of all the records in the system are:

        00000
        00011
        01101
        10100
        11111

In response to an arbitrary query q, what are the minimum and maximum numbers of these records the system could list?

	Minimum	Maximum
(A)	0	2
(B)	0	1
(C)	1	2
(D)	0	3
(E)	1	5

SAMPLE QUESTIONS ANSWER KEY

Software Systems and Methodology

1. D	13. D
2. B	14. C
3. A	15. E
4. D	16. C
5. C	17. D
6. A	18. A
7. B	19. C
8. D	20. D
9. E	21. D
10. D	22. C
11. A	23. B
12. C	24. C

Computer Organization and Architecture

25. C
26. C
27. B
28. C
29. D
30. B
31. B
32. B
33. A
34. B
35. B
36. A

Theory

37. C
38. B
39. A
40. D
41. E
42. C
43. A
44. A
45. D
46. E
47. E
48. C
49. D

Mathematical Background

50. D
51. B
52. B
53. E
54. E
55. C
56. E
57. C
58. D
59. D
60. C
61. E

Advanced Topics

62. D
63. B
64. A

TAKING THE TEST
TEST-TAKING STRATEGY

Presumably, if you are about to take the GRE Computer Science Test, you are nearing completion of or have completed an undergraduate curriculum in that subject. A general review of your curriculum is probably the best preparation for taking the test. Because the level of difficulty of the test is set to provide reliable measurement over a broad range of subject matter, you are not expected to be able to answer every question correctly.

You are strongly urged to work through some of the sample questions preceding this section. After you have evaluated your performance within the content categories, you may determine that a review of certain courses would be to your benefit.

In preparing to take the full-length Computer Science Test, it is important that you become thoroughly familiar with the directions provided in the full-length test included in this book. For this test, your score will be determined by subtracting one-fourth the number of incorrect answers from the number of correct answers. Questions for which you mark no answer or more than one answer are not counted in scoring. If you have some knowledge of a question and are able to rule out one or more of the answer choices as incorrect, your chances of selecting the correct answer are improved, and answering such questions is likely to improve your score. It is unlikely that pure guessing will raise your score; it may lower your score.

Work as rapidly as you can without being careless. *This includes checking frequently to make sure you are marking your answers in the appropriate rows on your answer sheet.* Since no question carries greater weight than any other, do not waste time pondering individual questions you find extremely difficult or unfamiliar.

You may find it advantageous to go through the test a first time quite rapidly, stopping only to answer those questions of which you are confident. Then go back and answer the questions that require greater thought, concluding with the very difficult questions, if you have time.

HOW TO SCORE YOUR TEST

Total Subject Test scores are reported as three-digit scaled scores with the third digit always zero. The maximum possible range for all Subject Test total scores is from 200 to 990. The actual range of scores for a particular Subject Test, however, may be smaller. Computer Science Test scores typically range from 420 to 860. The range for different editions of a given test may vary because different editions are not of precisely the same difficulty. The differences in ranges among different editions of a given test, however, usually are small. This should be taken into account, especially when comparing two very high scores. In general, differences between scores at the 99th percentile should be ignored. **The score conversions table provided shows the score range for this edition of the test only.**

The work sheet on page 39 lists the correct answers to the questions. Columns are provided for you to mark whether you chose the correct (C) answer or an incorrect (I) answer to each question. Draw a line across any question you omitted, because it is not counted in the scoring. At the bottom of the page, enter the total number correct and the total number incorrect. Divide the total incorrect by 4 and subtract the resulting number from the total correct. This is the adjustment made for guessing. Then round the result to the nearest whole number. This will give you your raw total score. Use the total score conversion table to find the scaled total score that corresponds to your raw total score.

Example: Suppose you chose the correct answers to 41 questions and incorrect answers to 34. Dividing 34 by 4 yields 8.5. Subtracting 8.5 from 41 equals 32.5, which is rounded to 33. The raw score of 33 corresponds to a scaled score of 670.

WORK SHEET for the COMPUTER SCIENCE Test, Form GR9129 ONLY
Answer Key and Percentages* of Examinees Answering Each Question Correctly

QUESTION Number	Answer	P+	TOTAL C	I	QUESTION Number	Answer	P+	TOTAL C	I
1	D	79			41	A	15		
2	B	76			42	D	63		
3	A	71			43	E	11		
4	D	30			44	D	67		
5	A	77			45	B	40		
6	D	49			46	C	38		
7	E	89			47	A	8		
8	A	56			48	C	62		
9	D	68			49	C	53		
10	B	30			50	C	53		
11	A	53			51	C	60		
12	B	15			52	B	30		
13	E	73			53	E	61		
14	E	51			54	B	18		
15	E	58			55	D	30		
16	A	51			56	E	32		
17	E	55			57	A	28		
18	C	46			58	E	40		
19	B	55			59	A	23		
20	E	51			60	D	34		
21	B	33			61	B	15		
22	D	35			62	B	39		
23	A	57			63	A	21		
24	C	60			64	D	10		
25	E	43			65	D	23		
26	D	66			66	C	33		
27	D	61			67	C	35		
28	B	78			68	B	12		
29	A	76			69	E	48		
30	E	38			70	B	11		
31	A	36			71	C	12		
32	E	22			72	C	25		
33	C	68			73	E	10		
34	A	19			74	E	42		
35	E	23			75	D	68		
36	A	43			76	D	32		
37	D	12			77	D	46		
38	C	40			78	A	22		
39	B	24			79	A	7		
40	E	61			80	D	43		

Correct (C) _____

Incorrect (I) _____

Total Score:

C – I/4 = _____

Scaled Score (SS) = _____

*The P+ column lists the percent of an analysis sample of Computer Science Test examinees who answered each question correctly; this sample consists of October 1990 examinees selected to represent all Computer Science Test examinees tested between October 1, 1987, and September 30, 1990.

SCORE CONVERSIONS AND PERCENTS BELOW*
FOR GRE COMPUTER SCIENCE TEST, Form GR9129 ONLY

TOTAL SCORE					
Raw Score	Scaled Score	%	Raw Score	Scaled Score	%
78-80	990	99	36	690	73
77	980	99	34-35	680	70
76	970	99	33	670	66
74-75	960	99	31-32	660	62
73	950	99	30	650	58
71-72	940	99	29	640	55
70	930	99	27-28	630	50
68-69	920	99	26	620	47
67	910	99	24-25	610	43
66	900	99	23	600	39
64-65	890	99	21-22	590	35
63	880	99	20	580	31
61-62	870	99	19	570	28
60	860	99	17-18	560	25
58-59	850	99	16	550	21
57	840	98	14-15	540	19
56	830	98	13	530	16
54-55	820	97	11-12	520	14
53	810	96	10	510	12
51-52	800	95	9	500	10
50	790	94	7-8	490	8
48-49	780	93	6	480	7
47	770	92	4-5	470	5
46	760	90	3	460	4
44-45	750	88	1-2	450	3
43	740	86	0	440	2
41-42	730	84			
40	720	81			
39	710	78			
37-38	700	76			

*Percent scoring below the scaled score based on the performance of 18,176 examinees who took the GRE Subject Test in Computer Science between October 1, 1987, and September 30, 1990.

EVALUATING YOUR PERFORMANCE

Now that you have scored your test, you may wish to compare your performance with the performance of others who took this test. Two kinds of information are provided, both using performance data from GRE Computer Science examinees tested between October 1987 and September 1990. Interpretive data based on the scores earned by examinees tested in this three-year period are to be used by admissions officers in 1991-92.

The first kind of information is based on the performance of a sample of the examinees who took the test in October 1990. This sample was selected to represent the total population of GRE Computer Science examinees tested between October 1987 and September 1990. On the work sheet you used to determine your score is a column labeled "P+." The numbers in this column indicate the percent of the examinees in this sample who answered each question correctly. You may use these numbers as a guide for evaluating your performance on each test question.

Also included, for each scaled score, is the percent of examinees tested between October 1987 and September 1990 who received lower scores. These percents appear in the score conversions table in a column to the right of the scaled scores. For example, in the percent column opposite the scaled score of 670 is the percent 66. This means that 66 percent of the Computer Science Test examinees tested between October 1987 and September 1990 scored lower than 670. To compare yourself with this population, look at the percent next to the scaled score you earned on the practice test. This number is a reasonable indication of your rank among GRE Computer Science Test examinees if you followed the test-taking suggestions in this practice book.

It is important to realize that the conditions under which you tested yourself were not exactly the same as those you will encounter at a test center. It is impossible to predict how different test-taking conditions will affect test performance, and this is only one factor that may account for differences between your practice test scores and your actual test scores. By comparing your performance on this practice test with the performance of other GRE Computer Science Test examinees, however, you will be able to determine your strengths and weaknesses and can then plan a program of study to prepare yourself for taking the Computer Science Test under standard conditions.

Before you start timing yourself on the test that follows, we suggest that you remove an answer sheet (pages 83 to 86) and turn first to the back cover of the test book (page 82), as you will do at the test center, and follow the instructions for completing the identification areas of the answer sheet. Then read the inside back cover instructions (page 81). When you are ready to begin the test, note the time and start marking your answers to the questions on the answer sheet.

**THE GRADUATE RECORD
EXAMINATIONS**

COMPUTER SCIENCE TEST

*Do not break the seal
until you are told to do so.*

*The contents of this test are confidential.
Disclosure or reproduction of any portion
of it is prohibited.*

THIS TEST BOOK MUST NOT BE TAKEN FROM THE ROOM.

Copyright © 1989, 1990 by Educational Testing Service. All rights reserved.
Princeton, N.J. 08541

COMPUTER SCIENCE TEST
Time—170 minutes
80 Questions

Notation and Conventions:

In this test a reading knowledge of Pascal-like languages is assumed. The following notational conventions are used.

1. All numbers are assumed to be written in decimal notation unless otherwise indicated.

2. $\lfloor x \rfloor$ denotes the greatest integer that is less than or equal to x.

3. $\lceil x \rceil$ denotes the least integer that is greater than or equal to x.

4. $g(n) = O(f(n))$ denotes "$g(n)$ has order at most $f(n)$" and means that there exist positive constants C and N such that $|g(n)| \le Cf(n)$ for all $n > N$.

    $g(n) = \Omega(f(n))$ denotes "$g(n)$ has order at least $f(n)$" and for this test means that there exist positive constants C and N such that $g(n) \ge Cf(n)$ for all $n > N$.

    $g(n) = \theta(f(n))$ denotes "$g(n)$ has the same order as $f(n)$" and means that there exist positive constants C_1, C_2, and N such that $C_1 f(n) \le g(n) \le C_2 f(n)$ for all $n > N$.

5. $\exists$ denotes "there exists."

    $\forall$ denotes "for all."

    $\Rightarrow$ denotes "implies."

    $\neg$ denotes "not"; "$\bar{A}$" is also used as meaning "$\neg A$."

    $\vee$ denotes "inclusive or"; $+$ also denotes "inclusive or."

    $\oplus$ denotes "exclusive or."

    $\wedge$ denotes "and"; also, juxtaposition of statements denotes "and," e.g., PQ denotes "P and Q."

    $\emptyset$ denotes the empty set.

6. If A and B denote sets, then:

    $A \cup B$ is the set of all elements that are in A or in B or in both;

    $A \cap B$ is the set of all elements that are in both A and B; AB also denotes $A \cap B$;

    $\bar{A}$ is the set of all elements not in A that are in some specified universal set.

7. In a string expression, if S and T denote strings or sets of strings, then:

    An empty string is denoted by ϵ or by Λ;

    ST denotes the concatenation of S and T;

    $S + T$ denotes $S \cup T$ or $\{S, T\}$, depending on context;

    S^n denotes $\underbrace{SS \ldots S}_{n \text{ factors}}$;

    S^* denotes $\epsilon + S + S^2 + S^3 + \ldots$;

    S^+ denotes $S + S^2 + S^3 + \ldots$.

GO ON TO THE NEXT PAGE.

8. In a grammar:

$\alpha \rightarrow \beta$ represents a production in the grammar.

$\alpha \Rightarrow \beta$ means β can be derived from α by the application of exactly one production.

$\alpha \overset{*}{\Rightarrow} \beta$ means β can be derived from α by the application of zero or more productions.

Unless otherwise specified

    (i)   symbols appearing on the left-hand side of productions are nonterminal symbols, the remaining symbols are terminal symbols,

    (ii) the leftmost symbol of the first production is the start symbol, and

    (iii) the start symbol is permitted to appear on the right-hand side of productions.

9. In a logic diagram:

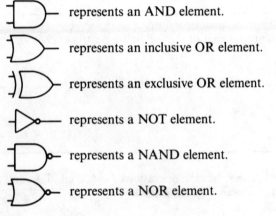

    represents an AND element.

    represents an inclusive OR element.

    represents an exclusive OR element.

    represents a NOT element.

    represents a NAND element.

    represents a NOR element.

10.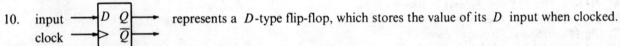

input   clock D Q $\overline{Q}$ represents a D-type flip-flop, which stores the value of its D input when clocked.

11. Binary tree traversal is defined recursively as follows:

    preorder - visit the root, traverse the left subtree, traverse the right subtree

    inorder   - traverse the left subtree, visit the root, traverse the right subtree

    postorder - traverse the left subtree, traverse the right subtree, visit the root

12. In a finite automaton diagram, states are represented by circles, with final (or accepting) states indicated by two concentric circles. The start state is indicated by the word "Start." An arc from state s to state t labeled a indicates a transition from s to t on input a. A label a/b indicates that this transition produces an output b. A label $a_1, a_2, \ldots, a_k$ indicates that the transition is made on any of the inputs $a_1, a_2, \ldots, a_k$.

GO ON TO THE NEXT PAGE.

Directions: Each of the questions or incomplete statements below is followed by five suggested answers or completions. Select the one that is best in each case and then fill in the corresponding space on the answer sheet.

1.

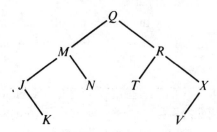

Which single node label of the tree above should be replaced so as to make the resulting tree a valid binary search tree?

(A) *J* (B) *M* (C) *Q* (D) *R* (E) *X*

2. The infix expression $A - (B + C) * (D / E)$ is equivalent to which of the following postfix expressions?

(A) *A B C* + − *D E* / *
(B) *A B C* + *D E* / * −
(C) *A B C* + * *D E* / −
(D) *A B C* + *D* / * *E* −
(E) *A B C* + *D E* / − *

3. Consider the following equations concerning a stack module that has the operations *Push*, *Pop*, *Top*, and *IsEmpty*. Which of the equations does NOT represent the conventional semantics of a stack?

(A) *IsEmpty(Push(Stack,Elem))* = *true*
(B) *Pop(Push(Stack,Elem))* = *Stack*
(C) *Top(Push(Stack,Elem))* = *Elem*
(D) *IsEmpty(Push(Push(Stack,Elem1),Elem2))* = *false*
(E) *Top(Pop(Push(Push(Stack,Elem1),Elem2)))* = *Elem1*

GO ON TO THE NEXT PAGE.

4. Which of the following pairs of 8-bit, two's-complement numbers will result in overflow when the members of the pairs are added?

   (A) 11111111, 00000001
   (B) 00000001, 10000000
   (C) 11111111, 10000001
   (D) 10000001, 10101010
   (E) 00111111, 00111111

---

5. An internal hash table has 5 buckets, numbered 0, 1, 2, 3, 4. Keys are integers, and the hash function

   $$h(i) = i \bmod 5$$

   is used, with linear resolution of collisions (i.e., if bucket $h(i)$ is filled, the buckets $h(i) + 1$, $h(i) + 2, \ldots$ are tried successively with all bucket numbers computed modulo 5). If elements with keys 13, 8, 24, 10, and 3 are inserted, in that order, into an initially blank hash table, then the content of the bucket numbered 2 is

   (A) 3   (B) 8   (C) 10   (D) 13   (E) 24

---

6. Which of the following sets of bit strings CANNOT be described with a regular expression?

   (A) All bit strings whose number of zeros is a multiple of five
   (B) All bit strings starting with a zero and ending with a one
   (C) All bit strings with an even number of zeros
   (D) All bit strings with more ones than zeros
   (E) All bit strings with no consecutive ones

GO ON TO THE NEXT PAGE.

7. Which of the following language features requires that stack-based storage allocation be used rather than static allocation?

    (A) Reference parameters
    (B) Integer-valued functions
    (C) Two-dimensional arrays
    (D) Arbitrary **goto**'s
    (E) Recursive procedures

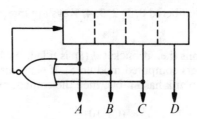

8. The figure above shows a 4-bit, right-shift register and a NOR gate. If the register outputs $\{ABCD\}$ at time 0 are 0110, then their values four clock pulses later are

    (A) 0100   (B) 0110   (C) 0111   (D) 1000   (E) 1111

GO ON TO THE NEXT PAGE.

Questions 9-10 refer to the following information.

A "trie" is a certain kind of tree that can be used to represent words (i.e., arbitrarily long but finite character strings) as follows.

(i) Each node of the trie is labeled with a single character; the root and all leaves are labeled with the special delimiter, * .

(ii) Every nonempty path through the trie from the root to a leaf represents the character string comprised of the sequence of characters encountered along that path.

(iii) No node has more than one leaf among its children, each leaf is the left-most child of its parent, and any nonleaf children appear from left to right in the order of their label.

Given an ordering for the alphabet of characters, every set of words uniquely determines a trie.

For example, the trie for "a", "an", "at", "and", and "cat" is drawn below.

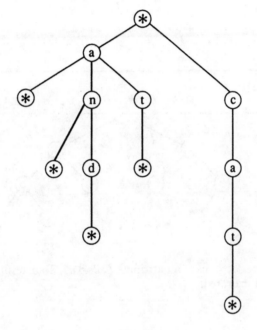

9. How many nodes (including * nodes) are there in the trie for "do", "dog", "door", and "doors" ?

(A) 8   (B) 9   (C) 10   (D) 11   (E) 12

10. Which of the following statements about the implementation of tries is NOT true?

(A) One expects to save space by using a trie to store a large collection of words because each unique prefix is stored just once.
(B) One can always print out an alphabetized list of the represented words in time that is linear in the number of nodes in the trie.
(C) Tries are of no particular advantage in storing sets of words with large numbers of common suffixes.
(D) Constant-time access from node to child can be achieved by using one link per character of the alphabet at each node.
(E) Tries can be represented in space proportional to the number of nodes in the trie.

GO ON TO THE NEXT PAGE.

11. Of the following page-replacement policies, which is guaranteed to incur the minimum number of page faults?

(A) Replace the page whose next reference will be the longest time in the future.
(B) Replace the page whose next reference will be the shortest time in the future.
(C) Replace the page whose most recent reference was the shortest time in the past.
(D) Replace the page whose most recent reference was the longest time in the past.
(E) Replace the page that has been referenced least frequently.

---

12. Which of the following statements describe(s) properties of a purely segmented memory system?

    I. It divides memory into units of equal size.
    II. It permits implementation of virtual memory.
    III. It suffers from internal fragmentation.

(A) I only
(B) II only
(C) III only
(D) I and III
(E) II and III

13.

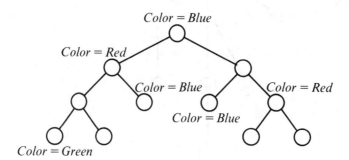

In the tree above, some of the nodes n have an attribute $Color(n)$. To determine a color for a given node n, the following pseudo-Pascal code is executed.

    function *FindColor*(n) : *Color* ;

    begin

      if n has attribute *Color* **then**

        FindColor := *Color*(n)

      else

        FindColor := *FindColor*(*Parent*(n))

    end ;

If *FindColor*(n) is evaluated for each node n of the tree above, how many of the 11 evaluations of *FindColor*(n) will result in *Red*?

(A) 2   (B) 3   (C) 4   (D) 5   (E) 6

GO ON TO THE NEXT PAGE.

50

14. Consider the following procedure, where *SetType* is an implementation for sets.

procedure *Insert*(*s* : *SetType*; *i* : *integer*);
(* Precondition: $i \notin s_0$, where s_0 denotes the value of *s*   *)
(* Postcondition: *s* is the union of s_0 and the singleton set $\{i\}$ *)

Which of the following statements is(are) true concerning the call *Insert*(*s*,*i*)?

    I. If the precondition is met, then, upon return from the call to *Insert*, the size of *s* will have increased by 1.
   II. The writer of any code that includes a call to *Insert* can assume *i* is not in *s* prior to the call.
  III. The writer of any code for the body of *Insert* can assume *i* is not in *s* upon entrance to the procedure.

(A) I only   (B) II only   (C) III only   (D) I and II   (E) I and III

---

15. In which of the following representations of numbers by 8-bit words is the addition of the integers 109 and -42 within range?

    I. One's complement
   II. Two's complement
  III. Sign and magnitude

(A) I only   (B) II only   (C) III only   (D) I and II only   (E) I, II, and III

GO ON TO THE NEXT PAGE.

51

Questions 16-17 refer to the following information.

In some database systems, data items are protected by locks to ensure correct behavior in the presence of concurrency. Locking is said to be "fine-grained" if each lock protects only a few data items; it is said to be "coarse-grained" if each lock protects many data items. The following performance graph is typical.

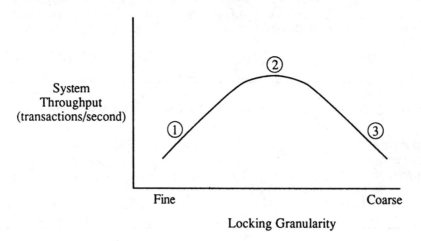

16. Between points 1 and 2, system throughput increases because

   (A) locking overhead decreases
   (B) locking overhead increases
   (C) fewer transactions desire to access data
   (D) greater concurrency is possible
   (E) less concurrency is possible

17. Between points 2 and 3, system throughput decreases because

   (A) locking overhead decreases
   (B) locking overhead increases
   (C) fewer transactions desire to access data
   (D) greater concurrency is possible
   (E) less concurrency is possible

GO ON TO THE NEXT PAGE.

18. A product-of-sums expression for the function $B\bar{D} + \bar{C}D$ is

(A) $(B + \bar{C})(\bar{D} + D)$

(B) $(B + \bar{D})(C + D)$

(C) $(B + D)(\bar{C} + \bar{D})$

(D) $(B + \bar{D})(\bar{C} + D)$

(E) $(B + D)(C + \bar{D})$

19.

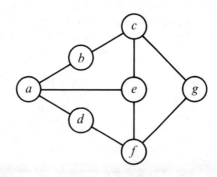

An independent set I of nodes of a graph G is a collection of nodes of G such that no two nodes of I are adjacent in G. A maximal independent set M of a graph G is an independent set such that if x is any node of G that is not in M, then $M \cup \{x\}$ is not an independent set. Which of the following is a maximal independent set of the graph in the figure above?

(A) $\{a, e\}$

(B) $\{a, g\}$

(C) $\{b, e, d\}$

(D) $\{b, e, g\}$

(E) $\{c, d, f\}$

GO ON TO THE NEXT PAGE.

20. A sequential circuit emits a 1 if and only if a 1 has just been received and the system has received an even number of 0's and an even number of 1's since it was reset. The system resets on emitting a 1. Which of the following is a possible state diagram for this circuit, where *A* is the initial (start) state?

(A)

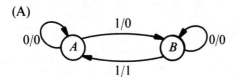

(B)

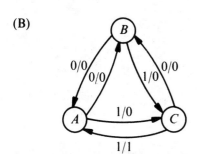

(C)

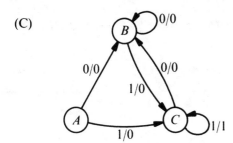

(D)

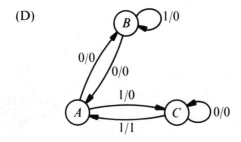

(E)   None of the above

---

21. Which of the following statements about circuits is(are) true?

   I. Combinational circuits may have feedback; sequential circuits do not.
  II. Combinational circuits have a "memoryless" property; sequential circuits do not.
 III. Both sequential and combinational circuits must be controlled by an external clock.

(A) I only
(B) II only
(C) I and II only
(D) II and III only
(E) I, II, and III

GO ON TO THE NEXT PAGE.

Questions 22-23 refer to the following information.

A simple (undirected or directed) graph is one in which there are no self loops and no multiple edges. An undirected graph is acyclic if it has no cycles. A directed graph is acyclic if it has no directed cycles.

22. What is the maximum possible number of directed edges in an n-node, simple, acyclic, <u>directed</u> graph?

(A) $n - 1$ (B) $3n$ (C) $\lfloor n/2 \rfloor * \lceil n/2 \rceil$ (D) $\binom{n}{2}$ (E) $n(n - 1)$

23. What is the maximum possible number of edges in an n-node, simple, acyclic, <u>undirected</u> graph?

(A) $n - 1$ (B) $3n$ (C) $\lfloor n/2 \rfloor * \lceil n/2 \rceil$ (D) $\binom{n}{2}$ (E) $n(n - 1)$

---

24. Suppose sharing of files in a multilevel directory structure is achieved with directory entries that are links pointing to a node containing information about a shared file. Information in this node includes (1) the owner of the file, (2) a count of the number of links to the file, and (3) the disk block numbers of the file. What is a primary drawback to this approach to sharing?

(A) If the owner modifies the file, another user who does not share will see the changes.
(B) If the owner renames the file, other users will not be able to access it.
(C) If the owner is allowed to delete a file, dangling links may result.
(D) If any user who shares the file appends to it, others who share it will not be able to access the new disk blocks.
(E) The system cannot know when blocks of a file can be reclaimed.

---

25. Which of the following considerations applies (apply) to choosing the page size in a paging system?
   I. An advantage of larger pages is that they lead to smaller page tables.
   II. An advantage of smaller pages is that they lead to less waste due to internal fragmentation.
   III. Normally, the dominant factor in disk access time is not dependent on page length, so longer pages can be used advantageously.

(A) I only   (B) II only   (C) I and III only   (D) II and III only   (E) I, II, and III

GO ON TO THE NEXT PAGE.

26. A <u>switch</u> is an element of the type

that connects p and t to r and s. The connections may be either straight (p to r; t to s) or crossed (p to s; t to r). The network below is used to connect four processors, A, B, C, D, to four memories, W, X, Y, Z.

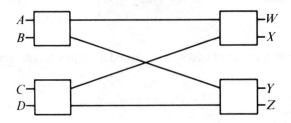

Which of the following connections can be achieved by some combination of switch settings?

   I. $A - X$, $B - Y$, $C - Z$, $D - W$
  II. $A - Y$, $B - Z$, $C - W$, $D - X$
 III. $A - Z$, $B - X$, $C - Y$, $D - W$

(A) I only   (B) II only   (C) III only   (D) I and III   (E) II and III

GO ON TO THE NEXT PAGE.

27. For a given problem with inputs of size n , two algorithms are run, one requiring time $c*n$ and the other requiring time $d*n^2$, where c and d are constants. Some measured running times of these algorithms are given below.

input size / algorithm	1024	2048
$c*n$	128	256
$d*n^2$	16	64

Which of the following can be correctly inferred from the information in the table?

(A) The information given is contradictory because a $c*n$ algorithm must always outperform a $d*n^2$ algorithm.
(B) The $c*n$ algorithm will outperform the $d*n^2$ algorithm only for n less than 16.
(C) The $c*n$ algorithm will begin to outperform the $d*n^2$ algorithm when n exceeds 4096.
(D) The $c*n$ algorithm will begin to outperform the $d*n^2$ algorithm when n exceeds 8192.
(E) The $c*n$ algorithm will never outperform the $d*n^2$ algorithm.

Questions 28-29 refer to the following information.

Suppose file protection in a system is represented by an access-rights matrix A , where $A(i, j)$ denotes the set of rights that user i has on file j . Users are divided into groups and may belong to more than one group. There are three modes of file access: (R)ead, (W)rite, and (E)xecute.

The system has three file types: Mail, Text, and Binary. Consider the following set of security policies.

1. Each user has R and W access to all files owned by that user, plus E access to Binary files owned by that user.
2. Users in the same group have E access to each other's Binary files, and R access to each other's Mail files, and R and W access to each other's Text files.
3. A Super User has access to all files as if all files were owned by the Super User.

28. Carol, Ted, and Alice are three users of the system. Carol and Alice are in the same group. Ted is a Super User. Which of the following rights is INCONSISTENT with the given policies?

(A) Ted has W access to Alice's Mail files.
(B) Ted has E access to Alice's Mail files.
(C) Carol has R access to Alice's Text files.
(D) Ted has E access to Carol's Binary files.
(E) Carol has R access to Carol's Mail files.

29. Which of the following pieces of security-policy information CANNOT be determined from an access-rights matrix?

(A) The number of groups to which a given user is allowed to belong
(B) Which users have E rights to a given file
(C) The files to which a given user does not have access rights
(D) Whether a given user who has R access to a given file also has W access to the same file
(E) The number of users who have R access to a given file

GO ON TO THE NEXT PAGE.

57

30. Consider the following postcondition for a routine that is supposed to sort an array $A[1..n]$ in nondecreasing order.

$$\text{"} 1 \leq i < n \text{ implies } A[i] \leq A[i + 1] \text{"}$$

Which of the following statements is true about this postcondition?

(A) It is too strong because it would not allow the routine to change A.
(B) It is incorrect and should be: "$...1 \leq i \leq n$ implies $A[i] \leq A[i + 1]$."
(C) It is incorrect and should be: "$...1 < i \leq n$ implies $A[i] < A[i + 1]$."
(D) It is appropriate because it implies that the set of values stored in the resulting array is a subset of the values stored in the initial array.
(E) It is too weak because it does not express the requirement that the resulting array be a permutation of the initial array.

---

31. Consider a computer system in which processes can request and release one or more resources. Once a process has been granted a resource, the process has exclusive use of that resource until it is released. If a process requests a resource that is already in use, the process enters a queue for that resource, waiting until the resource is available. Which of the following will NOT deal effectively with the problem of deadlock?

(A) Giving priorities to processes and ordering the wait queues by priority
(B) Having a process request all its required resources when it first begins, and restarting if it cannot obtain them all
(C) Numbering the resources and requiring that processes request resources in order of increasing number
(D) Having processes time out and restart after a random interval of waiting
(E) Having the operating system monitor the wait queues and restart processes to break deadlocks

---

32. A 3-way, set-associative cache is

(A) more complex than a 4-way, set-associative cache
(B) faster to access than a direct-mapped cache
(C) possible only with write-back
(D) effective only if 3 or fewer processes are running alternately on the processor
(E) one in which each main memory word can be stored at any of 3 cache locations

---

GO ON TO THE NEXT PAGE.

33.
$$S \rightarrow aSb \mid bSa \mid SS \mid \epsilon$$

Which of the following best characterizes the language generated by the grammar above?

(A) All strings of the form $a^i b^j a^k$, where $i + j = k$
(B) All palindromes over a and b
(C) All strings with equal numbers of a's and b's
(D) All strings of the form ww^R, where $w \in \{a, b\}^*$
(E) All even-length strings of a's and b's

---

34. Which of the following statements is FALSE about memory reclamation based on reference counting?

(A) Reference counting is well suited for reclaiming cyclic structures.
(B) Reference counting incurs additional space overhead for each memory cell.
(C) Reference counting is an alternative to mark-and-sweep garbage collection.
(D) Reference counting need not keep track of which cells point to other cells.
(E) Time to reclaim could be linear in the number of cells to be reclaimed.

---

35. Which of the following evaluation strategies must be defined in order to execute a logic program on a sequential machine?

    I. Evaluation order of rules
   II. Evaluation order of clauses
  III. Evaluation order of arguments in each clause

(A) II only
(B) I and II only
(C) I and III only
(D) II and III only
(E) I, II, and III

GO ON TO THE NEXT PAGE.

36. Consider an object-oriented language in which all entities are objects. Two relationships arise: (1) the *instance* relationship, between an object and the class of which that object is a member, and (2) the *subclass* relationship, between a class and the superclass from which that class inherits properties. In such a language, when a message is sent to an object requesting execution of one of its methods (procedures), the method is located by following

    (A) one instance link and then zero or more subclass links
    (B) one or more instance links and then one or more subclass links
    (C) one or more instance links
    (D) one or more subclass links
    (E) one subclass link and then one or more instance links

---

37. Suppose it takes 1 second to factor a general 100×100 matrix using Gaussian elimination. Of the following, which is the best estimate of the number of seconds it will take to factor a 500×500 matrix based on the relative dimensions?

    (A)   5
    (B) 10
    (C) 25
    (D) 125
    (E) 625

---

38. At time 0, five jobs are available for execution on a single processor, with service times of 25, 15, 5, 3, and 2 time units. Which of the following is the minimum value of the average completion time of these jobs?

    (A) 50   (B) 208/5   (C) 92/5   (D) 10   (E) 5

GO ON TO THE NEXT PAGE.

39. Consider the representation of the array

> **var** A: **array**[$L1..U1, L2..U2$] **of** *integer* ;

on a word-addressable machine on which arrays are stored in row-major order and integers occupy one word. The location of $A[I, J]$ can be calculated as follows.

$$Loc(A[I, J]) = Loc(A[L1, L2]) + (I - L1)*Multiplier_1 + (J - L2)*Multiplier_2$$

where $Multiplier_i$ is the number of words between elements whose subscripts differ by 1 in dimension i. The "origin" of an array is $Loc(A[L1, L2])$. To reduce the number of run-time subtractions, it is useful to calculate a "virtual origin," defined as $Loc(A[0, 0])$ (whether or not this element exists in the actual array).

The virtual origin of the array

> **var** A: **array**[$-3..2, 5..7$] **of** *integer*

is

(A) $Loc(A[-3, 5]) + 14$
(B) $Loc(A[-3, 5]) + 4$
(C) $Loc(A[-3, 5]) - 3$
(D) $Loc(A[-3, 5]) - 14$
(E) $Loc(A[-3, 5]) - 21$

GO ON TO THE NEXT PAGE.

Questions 40-41 are based on the following information.

A graph of n nodes numbered $1, 2, \ldots, n$ can be represented by $n \times n$ adjacency matrix G, where

$$G[i,j] = \begin{cases} true, & \text{if there is an edge connecting nodes } i \text{ and } j \\ false, & \text{otherwise} \end{cases}$$

The following procedure replaces Boolean matrix A by the logical sum of A and its square; e.g., if A is an adjacency matrix representing a graph, then the procedure adds edges where there are paths of length 2.

```
     type
         Matrix = array [1..n, 1..n] of Boolean ;
     procedure PlusSquare (var A : Matrix) ;
       var
         B       : Matrix ;
         i, j, k : integer ;
       begin {Compute B = A² + A}
       for i := 1 to n do
         for j := 1 to n do
           begin
             B[i,j] := A[i,j] ;
             for k := 1 to n do
               if A[i,k] and A[k,j] then
(*1*)              B[i,j] := true

           end ;
       {Now copy B into A}
       for i := 1 to n do
         for j := 1 to n do

           A[i,j] := B[i,j]
     end ;
```

GO ON TO THE NEXT PAGE.

40. Which of the following best indicates the maximum number of times that the assignment statement

$B[i, j] := true$ (marked 1 in the procedure)

can be executed?

(A) $O(\log n)$ (B) $O(n)$ (C) $O(n \log n)$ (D) $O(n^2)$ (E) $O(n^3)$

41. The transitive closure of the graph G is an $n \times n$ matrix T such that

$$T[i, j] = \begin{cases} true, \text{ if there is a path of length 1 or more from } i \text{ to } j \\ false, \text{ otherwise.} \end{cases}$$

The following procedure uses **procedure** *PlusSquare* to compute the transitive closure of graph G by means of a **for**-loop iterated k times, where k is determined by n.

procedure *Closure* (**var** A : *matrix*) ;
  var
    i : *integer* ;
begin
  for $i := 1$ **to** k **do**
    PlusSquare(A)
end ;

Of the following, which is the best approximation to the smallest value of k for which the call

    Closure(G)

can be guaranteed to compute the transitive closure of G ?

(A) $\log_2 n$ (B) n (C) $n \log_2 n$ (D) n^2 (E) n^3

GO ON TO THE NEXT PAGE.

42. A compiler generates code for the following assignment statement.

$$G := (A + B) * C - (D + E) * F$$

The target machine has a single accumulator and a single-address instruction set consisting of instructions load, store, add, subtract, and multiply. For the arithmetic operations, the left operand is taken from the accumulator and the result appears in the accumulator. The smallest possible number of instructions in the resulting code is

(A) 5   (B) 6   (C) 7   (D) 9   (E) 11

43. Consider the following directed graph.

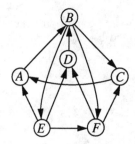

This graph has six vertices (labeled *A-F*) and eleven directed edges *AB*, *BC*, *BE*, *BF*, *CA*, *DB*, *EA*, *ED*, *EF*, *FC*, and *FD*. Which of the following properties does this graph have?

   I. It has a planar embedding.
  II. It is strongly connected.
 III. It has a directed Hamiltonian path starting at *C*.

(A) I only
(B) II only
(C) III only
(D) II and III only
(E) I, II, and III

GO ON TO THE NEXT PAGE.

Questions 44-45 refer to the following information.

In the following form of binary search one can determine whether some particular integer x is present in a sorted (in ascending order) array $a[L..R]$ using the following steps in the order shown.

Let $M = (L + R)$ **div** 2.
If $x = a[M]$, then terminate (success).
If $x < a[M]$ and $M > L$, use the same algorithm on $a[L..M - 1]$.
If $x > a[M]$ and $M < R$, use the same algorithm on $a[M + 1..R]$.
Otherwise terminate (failure).

44. Which of the following statements is (are) true about binary search in $a[1..N]$, where N is a large positive integer?

    I. If x is present in $a[1..N]$, then x is always found within $O(log N)$ comparisons.
    II. If x is not present in $a[1..N]$, then failure is always reached within $O(log N)$ comparisons.
    III. Searching for two different values of x, neither of which is present in $a[1..N]$, always takes the same number of steps to determine failure.

(A) I only   (B) II only   (C) III only   (D) I and II   (E) II and III

45. Suppose that the first step in the binary search algorithm given above is changed to

"Let $M = (3L + R)$ **div** 4."

What effect does this have on the worst-case number of comparisons for searching in $a[1..N]$, where N is a large positive integer?

(A) The number of comparisons is changed at most by an additive constant.
(B) The number of comparisons is somewhat more than doubled.
(C) The number of comparisons is roughly halved.
(D) The number of comparisons could be as large as N.
(E) The number of comparisons is not affected.

---

46. Which of the following statements about floating-point arithmetic is NOT true?

(A) It is inherently nonassociative because some numbers have no exact representation.
(B) It is inherently nonassociative because there have to be upper and lower bounds on the size of numbers.
(C) Associativity can be achieved with appropriate roundoff conventions.
(D) Some rational numbers have no exact representation.
(E) No irrational number has an exact representation.

GO ON TO THE NEXT PAGE.

47. Consider the following functions written in a procedural language.

```
function F(i, k);
begin
  if i = 0 then
    F := 1
  else
    F := k
end;
function G(x);
begin
  G := F(x, x * G(x − 1))
end;
```

Under which parameter-passing mechanism will G terminate as a result of the call $G(5)$?

(A) Call-by-name
(B) Call-by-value
(C) Call-by-value-result
(D) Call-by-reference
(E) Call-by-need

---

48. Assume that any assignment statement can be executed in unit time. If as many identical processors as needed are used, what is the minimum number of time units needed to execute the assignments

$$A := B + C$$
$$B := A − B$$
$$C := A * E$$
$$D := A/F$$
$$E := B − C$$
$$F := A + B$$

with the same result as if the assignments were executed in the order shown?

(A) 1   (B) 2   (C) 3   (D) 4   (E) 5

GO ON TO THE NEXT PAGE.

Questions 49-50 refer to the following information.

Consider the following table showing a set of jobs to be processed on a single processor, the number of seconds of service that each requires, and each job's arrival time.

Job	Service Time (sec.)	Arrival time
1	2	t_0
2	5	t_0
3	1	$t_0 + 1$ sec.
4	9	$t_0 + 5$ sec.
5	3	$t_0 + 10$ sec.
6	2	$t_0 + 15$ sec.

49. If a round-robin scheduling algorithm with a time slice of 10 milliseconds is assumed, then at approximately what time is Job 3 completed?

(A) $t_0 + 22$ sec.
(B) $t_0 + 8$ sec.
(C) $t_0 + 4$ sec.
(D) $t_0 + 2$ sec.
(E) $t_0 + 1$ sec.

50. If a first-come-first-served scheduling algorithm is assumed, where ties are resolved in favor of the smaller-numbered job, what is the average (arithmetic mean) number of seconds that a job waits before being assigned to the processor?

(A) 20/6
(B) 21/6
(C) 23/6
(D) 31/6
(E) 54/6

GO ON TO THE NEXT PAGE.

51. A grammar is said to be "useless" if and only if it produces no terminal strings. If S is the start symbol, which of the following grammars is (are) "useless"?

    I. $S \rightarrow AB|AS$
       $A \rightarrow B|a$
       $B \rightarrow A|b$

    II. $S \rightarrow SA|AS|SB$
       $A \rightarrow a$
       $B \rightarrow a|b$

    III. $S \rightarrow \epsilon|A$
       $A \rightarrow B$
       $B \rightarrow C$
       $C \rightarrow a$

(A) None   (B) I only   (C) II only   (D) III only   (E) I, II, and III

GO ON TO THE NEXT PAGE.

Questions 52-53 refer to the following Pascal-like program and to two possible scoping rules that can be used to resolve variable references. With <u>static</u> scoping (references resolvable in the defining environment, e.g., at compile time), a variable reference is to the declaration in the smallest enclosing block; with <u>dynamic</u> scoping (references resolvable in the calling environment), a variable reference is to the declaration in the most recently executed block.

```
program Main (output) ;
var x: integer ;
  procedure p1 ;
    procedure p2 ;
    var x : integer ;
      begin
        x := 0 ;
        p1
      end ;
    begin {p1}
      while x < 2 do
        begin
          write(x) ;
          x := x + 1 ;
          p2
        end ;
      write(x)
    end ; {p1}
  begin {Main}
    x := 0 ;
    p1
  end.
```

52. What is the output of the program shown above if it is assumed that references to nonlocal variables are resolved using static scoping?

(A) 0 1 2 2
(B) 0 1 2 2 2
(C) The program will not compile because it contains a use of an undeclared variable.
(D) The output cannot be determined because the program uses the value of an uninitialized variable.
(E) The output of the program is infinite because the program includes an infinite recursion.

53. What is the output of the program shown above if it is assumed that references to nonlocal variables are resolved using dynamic scoping?

(A) 0 1 2
(B) 0 0 1 2 2
(C) The program will not compile because it contains a use of an undeclared variable.
(D) The output cannot be determined because the program uses the value of an uninitialized variable.
(E) The output of the program is infinite because the program includes an infinite recursion.

GO ON TO THE NEXT PAGE.

54.

$$
\begin{array}{ccccc}
0 & 0 & 0 & 1 & 0 \\
0 & 1 & 0 & 1 & 1 \\
0 & 1 & 1 & 0 & 1 \\
1 & 0 & 0 & 0 & 1 \\
1 & 1 & 1 & 1 & 1
\end{array}
$$

The set of five binary words shown as rows above is used as a code. Because of channel noise, any sequence of five bits could be received. A code is said to be able to correct all k-bit errors if no received word can have Hamming distance k or less from two different code words. (The Hamming distance between two binary words is the number of bit positions in which they differ.) A code is said to be able to detect all k-bit errors if no code word is at a Hamming distance of k or less from any other code word. Which of the following is true of the code above?

(A) It cannot detect all 1-bit errors.
(B) It can detect all 1-bit errors but cannot correct all 1-bit errors.
(C) It can correct all 1-bit errors but cannot detect all 2-bit errors.
(D) It can detect all 2-bit errors but cannot correct all 2-bit errors.
(E) It can correct all 2-bit errors.

Questions 55-57 refer to the following recursive program.

function $X(N : integer) : integer$;

begin

  if $N < 3$ **then**

    $X := 1$

  else

    $X := X(N - 1) + X(N - 3) + 1$

end ;

55. How many times is the function X called when $X(X(5))$ is evaluated?

(A) 7   (B) 14   (C) 16   (D) 24   (E) 30

56. As a function of N, which of the following best describes the running time of this function when invoked with the call $X(N)$?

(A) Linear   (B) Quadratic   (C) Cubic   (D) Logarithmic   (E) Exponential

57. As a function of $X(N)$, which of the following best describes the running time of this function when invoked with the call $X(N)$?

(A) Linear   (B) Quadratic   (C) Cubic   (D) Logarithmic   (E) Exponential

---

GO ON TO THE NEXT PAGE.

58.

```
C1:    i := 1 ;                    C2:    a := 3 ;
       while i <= n do                    i := 5 * n ;
         begin                            x := 5 ;
           a := 3 ;                       while x <= i do
           writeln(5 * i) ;                 begin
           i := i + 1                         writeln(x) ;
         end                                  x := x + 5
                                            end
```

Which of the following conditions is (are) necessary to assure that program fragment C2 above can replace program fragment C1 within an otherwise arbitrary program without changing what the surrounding program does?

   I. x is dead (its value will not subsequently be needed) on exit from the **while** loop.
   II. $n \geq 1$ on entry to the **while** loops.
   III. i is dead on exit from the **while** loops.

(A) II only   (B) III only   (C) I and II only   (D) II and III only   (E) I, II, and III

---

59. If $p(x)$ is the minimal-degree interpolating polynomial for the real-valued function $f(x)$ at the $n + 1$ distinct real numbers $x_0, \ldots, x_n$, what is the maximum possible degree of $p(x)$?

(A) n (B) $n + 1$ (C) $n + 2$ (D) $2n$ (E) $2n + 1$

---

60. "Magic memory" has two operations: *Read* and *Clear*. Both are indivisible and mutually exclusive. *Clear* sets the magic memory to zero. *Read* returns a value that represents the number of *Read* operations since the last *Clear* operation. Which of the following is(are) true of "Magic memory"?

   I. It can provide the functionality of an atomic *Test-and-Set*.
   II. It can be used to coordinate processes running on a shared-memory multiprocessor.
   III. It is only useful on a multiprocessor.

(A) I only   (B) II only   (C) III only   (D) I and II   (E) II and III

GO ON TO THE NEXT PAGE.

61. I. $(P \Rightarrow \neg P)$
 II. $((P \Rightarrow \neg P) \text{ or } (\neg P \Rightarrow P))$

Which of the following characterizes the nature of the formulas above?

(A) I is unsatisfiable; II is valid.
(B) I is satisfiable but not valid; II is valid.
(C) Both I and II are satisfiable, but neither is valid.
(D) Both I and II are unsatisfiable.
(E) I is unsatisfiable; II is satisfiable but not valid.

---

62. A multiplexor, shown below on the right, has six inputs, S_0, S_1, A, B, C, and D. The truth table on the left describes its function.

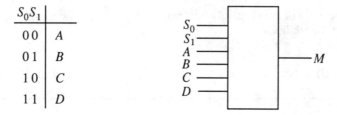

$S_0 S_1$	
0 0	A
0 1	B
1 0	C
1 1	D

It is desired to implement the function $F = (X \oplus Y) \oplus Z$ using the multiplexor. If X is applied to S_0 and Y is applied to S_1, what inputs should be applied to A, B, C, and D to realize the function F?

(A) $A = X + Y$, $B = X + Z$, $C = Y + Z$, $D = Z$

(B) $A = D = Z$, $B = C = \bar{Z}$

(C) $A = X \oplus Y$, $B = X \oplus Z$, $C = Y \oplus Z$, $D = Z$

(D) $A = B = C = D = Z$

(E) The function F cannot be realized with any of the inputs shown above.

GO ON TO THE NEXT PAGE.

63. Function signatures describe the types of the arguments to a function as well as the return value of the function. For instance, the addition function on reals has a signature of

$$add : real \times real \to real$$

since it takes two real numbers and returns a real number. But, for a language that allows functions as return values, addition could be considered to have the signature

$$add : real \to (real \to real)$$

which means that *add* takes a single real (the first operand) and returns a new function that itself takes a single real (the second operand) and returns a real (the result). This process of reducing a function with multiple arguments to a function with fewer arguments is called <u>currying</u>. Which of the following is correct?

(A) Currying can be applied to any function to the point where it has exactly one input argument.
(B) Currying cannot be applied to functions of more than two arguments.
(C) Currying cannot be applied to functions that return functions as arguments.
(D) Currying cannot be applied to functions that have arguments that are functions.
(E) Currying can be applied only to functions that are associative.

---

64. If $T(0) = T(1) = 1$, each of the following recurrences for $n \geq 2$ defines a function T on the nonnegative integers. Which CANNOT be bounded by a polynomial function?

(A) $T(n) = 3T(\lfloor n/2 \rfloor) + n^2$

(B) $T(n) = 4T(\lfloor n/2 \rfloor) + n$

(C) $T(n) = T(\lfloor 7n/8 \rfloor) + 8n + 1$

(D) $T(n) = 2T(n - 2) + 1$

(E) $T(n) = T(n - 1) + n^2$

---

65. Which of the following sets of productions determine(s) an ambiguous context-free grammar?

I. $<stmt> \to$ **if** $<cond>$ **then** $<stmt>$
   $<stmt> \to$ **if** $<cond>$ **then** $<stmt>$ **else** $<stmt>$
   $<stmt> \to$ **skip**
   $<cond> \to$ **true** | **false**

II. $<stmt> \to$ **if** $<cond>$ **then** $<stmt>$ **fi**
   $<stmt> \to$ **if** $<cond>$ **then** $<stmt>$ **else** $<stmt>$ **fi**
   $<stmt> \to$ **skip**
   $<cond> \to$ **true** | **false**

III. $<stmt> \to$ **if** $<cond>$ **then** $<stmt>$ $<tail>$
   $<stmt> \to$ **skip**
   $<cond> \to$ **true** | **false**
   $<tail> \to \epsilon$
   $<tail> \to$ **else** $<stmt>$

(A) I only   (B) II only   (C) II and III only   (D) I and III only   (E) I, II, and III

GO ON TO THE NEXT PAGE.

66. The hit ratio of a cache memory is the percentage of accesses (reads and writes) for which data are found in the cache. Write-through is a policy whereby every write operation updates main memory. Write-back is a policy whereby a write operation to a line found in the cache does not affect main memory until the line is evicted from the cache. Write-allocation is a policy whereby a cache line is allocated and loaded on a write-miss. If it is assumed that write-allocation is always used, which of the following is true?

(A) Write-back usually results in a better hit ratio than write-through.
(B) Write-through usually results in a better hit ratio than write-back.
(C) The percentage of write operations resulting in a main memory operation will never be larger for write-back than for write-through.
(D) The percentage of write operations resulting in a main memory operation will never be larger for write-through than for write-back.
(E) Write-through can only be employed in a set-associative cache.

67.

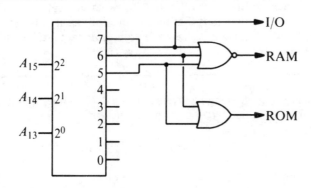

The 64k address space of a certain microcomputer is accessed by address signals A_0, A_1, . . . , A_{14}, A_{15} (where A_0 is the least significant bit and A_{15} is the most significant bit) and is divided unequally among read-only memory (ROM), read-write memory (RAM), and input-output registers (I/O) by means of the decoder and gates shown above. Note that only the three high-order outputs of the decoder are used. Output i ($0 \leq i \leq 7$) of the decoder is 1 if and only if the binary value of the inputs $A_{15}A_{14}A_{13}$ is i. Which of the following correctly indicates the beginning and ending hexadecimal addresses of the three portions of the address space?

	ROM	RAM	I/O
(A)	0000 - 3FFF	4000 - DFFF	E000 - FFFF
(B)	0000 - 9FFF	A000 - DFFF	E000 - FFFF
(C)	A000 - DFFF	0000 - 9FFF	E000 - FFFF
(D)	4000 - 4FFF	6000 - FFFF	0000 - 3FFF
(E)	E000 - FFFF	4000 - DFFF	0000 - 3FFF

GO ON TO THE NEXT PAGE.

74

68. Which of the following statements about horizontal versus vertical microarchitecture is (are) true?

    I. Programs for horizontal architectures require more time steps than those for vertical architectures.
    II. Horizontal microinstructions are unencoded.
    III. Horizontal microinstructions usually have a single opcode and multiple operand specifiers.

(A) I only   (B) II only   (C) III only   (D) II and III only   (E) I, II, and III

69.

$\overset{CD}{AB}$	00	01	11	10
00	x	x	1	x
01	0	0	1	0
11	1	1	x	x
10	1	0	1	1

The Karnaugh map shown above illustrates a switching function $f(A, B, C, D)$ that includes five "don't cares." Which of the following expressions is (are) valid representations of f?

    I. $AB \vee CD \vee A\bar{D}$

    II. $AB \vee CD \vee \bar{B}\bar{D}$

    III. $(B \vee C \vee \bar{D})(A \vee C)(A \vee D)$

(A) I only   (B) II only   (C) I and III only   (D) II and III only   (E) I, II, and III

GO ON TO THE NEXT PAGE.

75

70. As a generating function, $\dfrac{1}{1 - 2z}$ generates the sequence 1, 2, 4, 8, 16, ... Which of the following is the generating function for the sequence 1, 1, 2, 2, 3, 3, 4, 4, 5, 5, . . . ?

(A) $\dfrac{1}{1 - z^2}$

(B) $\dfrac{1}{(1 - z)(1 - z^2)}$

(C) $\dfrac{1}{1 - z}$

(D) $\dfrac{1}{1 - 3z}$

(E) $\dfrac{1}{1 - z} + \dfrac{1}{1 - z^2}$

---

71. Resolution theorem proving for showing that a formula of propositional logic is not satisfiable has which of the following properties?

   I. It is a sound proof system in the sense that there does not exist a proof of the unsatisfiability of a satisfiable formula of propositional logic.
   II. It is a complete proof system in the sense that there is a proof of unsatisfiability for every unsatisfiable formula of propositional logic.
   III. It is a succinct proof system in the sense that whenever an unsatisfiable formula F of propositional logic has a resolution proof, F also has a proof whose length is polynomial in the length of F.

(A) I only   (B) III only   (C) I and II only   (D) I and III only   (E) I, II, and III

GO ON TO THE NEXT PAGE.

72. A "strictly binary tree" is a binary tree in which every node that is not a leaf has two children. Suppose that for a class of strictly binary trees there exists $c > 0$ such that, for any tree in the class, the ratio of the lengths of any two root-to-leaf paths is bounded above by c. Which of the following best characterizes the height h of any tree in this class, where N is the number of nodes in the tree and $N > 1$?

(A) $h \leq log_2(N)$

(B) $h = 1/c\ log_2(N)$

(C) $h < c\ log_2(N)$

(D) $h > c\ log_2(N)$

(E) $h \leq log_2(cN)$

73. If the cube root of 7 is approximated by applying Newton's method to the function $f(x) = x^3 - 7$, with initial value x_0 and successive approximations $x_1, x_2, x_3, \ldots$, which of the following is(are) true?

   I. If $x_0 = 2$, then $|x_{10} - \sqrt[3]{7}| < 10^{-16}$.

   II. If $x_0 = 2$, then the method converges faster than the bisection method with initial endpoint values 1 and 3.

   III. If $x_0 > 0$, then the method will converge.

(A) II only   (B) III only   (C) I and II only   (D) I and III only   (E) I, II, and III

74. For all strings x, the function x^M is defined recursively as follows.

$\epsilon^M = \epsilon$, and

if w is a string and a is a string with length 1, then

$(aw)^M = aw^M a$.

Let a be a string with length 1, and let x and y be arbitrary strings. Which of the following is true?

(A) $a^M = a$

(B) $(ax)^M = (xa)^M$

(C) $(xy)^M = y^M x^M$

(D) $(xy)^M = xy^M x$

(E) None of the above

GO ON TO THE NEXT PAGE.

Questions 75-76 are based on the following information.

As shown in the three diagrams below, device *FA* makes use of two copies of device *HA*, and device *D* makes use of four copies of device *FA*. Assume that all gates have the same delay *T*.

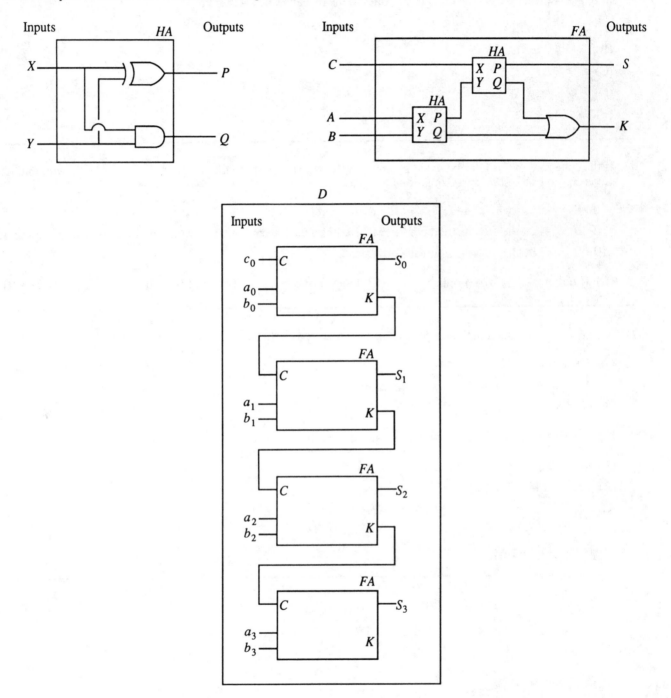

GO ON TO THE NEXT PAGE.

75. If all inputs to device D become available simultaneously, which output will be available last?

(A) S_0
(B) S_1
(C) S_2
(D) S_3
(E) They will all be available simultaneously.

76. If all inputs to device D become available simultaneously, what is the delay before S_2 must be valid?

(A) $2T$
(B) $3T$
(C) $4T$
(D) $6T$
(E) $9T$

---

77. If $x = 3^{(5^{64})} \bmod 7$ and $y = 3^{(5^{64})} \bmod 9$, which of the following is true?

(A) $(x + y) \bmod 63 \neq (y + x) \bmod 63$
(B) $x \bmod 63 = y \bmod 63$
(C) $(xy) \bmod 63 \neq (yx) \bmod 63$
(D) There exists z such that $z \bmod 7 = x$ and $z \bmod 9 = y$.
(E) There exists z such that $(yz) \bmod 63 = 1$.

---

78. Many cryptographic protocols base their security on assumptions about the computational difficulty of integer factorization. Integer factorization serves this purpose because we believe that

(A) integer multiplication is a function whose inverse, factorization, remains difficult for a large class of inputs
(B) $P = NP$
(C) even if $P = NP$, integer factorization is still likely not to be polynomial-time computable
(D) testing primality is computationally intractable
(E) integer factorization is NP-hard

GO ON TO THE NEXT PAGE.

79. Consider the following grammars, each with start symbol S.

$$G_1 : S \to A \qquad\qquad G_2 : S \to A$$
$$A \to aAb \mid ab \qquad\qquad A \to aA \mid a \mid \epsilon$$

Which of the following statements is true?

(A) G_1 is $LR(0)$; but, for any k, G_2 is not $LR(k)$.
(B) G_2 is $LR(0)$; but, for any k, G_1 is not $LR(k)$.
(C) G_2 is $LR(2)$; but, for any k, G_1 is not $LR(k)$.
(D) For any k, neither G_1 nor G_2 is $LR(k)$.
(E) G_1 and G_2 are both $LR(1)$.

80.

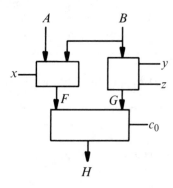

The figure above shows part of a CPU with parallel data paths A, B, F, G, and H. The information on these paths is interpreted as integers in two's-complement notation. The four control signals x, y, z, and (the low-order carry-in) c_0, come from a control unit and cause the boxes in the figure to implement the following functions:

$$F = \bar{x}A \vee xB; \ G = yB \oplus z; \ H = F + G + c_0$$

where $\vee$ is bit-wise OR, $\oplus$ is bit-wise exclusive OR, the bit-wise AND is denoted by juxtaposition, and $+$ is arithmetic plus.

Which of the following values of H CANNOT be realized by some combination of the control signals and c_0 ?

(A) A (B) B (C) $A + B + 1$ (D) $A - B + 1$ (E) $A - B$

IF YOU FINISH BEFORE TIME IS CALLED, YOU MAY CHECK YOUR WORK ON THIS TEST.

COMPUTER SCIENCE TEST

Time—170 minutes

80 Questions

The Subject Tests are intended to measure your achievement in a specialized field of study. Most of the questions are concerned with subject matter that is probably familiar to you, but some of the questions may refer to areas that you have not studied.

Your score will be determined by subtracting one-fourth the number of incorrect answers from the number of correct answers. Questions for which you mark no answer or more than one answer are not counted in scoring. If you have some knowledge of a question and are able to rule out one or more of the answer choices as incorrect, your chances of selecting the correct answer are improved, and answering such questions will likely improve your score. It is unlikely that pure guessing will raise your score; it may lower your score.

You are advised to use your time effectively and to work as rapidly as you can without losing accuracy. Do not spend too much time on questions that are too difficult for you. Go on to the other questions and come back to the difficult ones later if you can.

YOU MUST INDICATE ALL YOUR ANSWERS ON THE SEPARATE ANSWER SHEET. No credit will be given for anything written in this examination book, but to work out your answers you may write in the book as much as you wish. After you have decided which of the suggested answers is best, fill in completely the corresponding space on the answer sheet. Be sure to:

- Use a soft black lead pencil (No. 2 or HB).

- Mark only one answer to each question. No credit will be given for multiple answers.

- Mark your answer in the row with the same number as the number of the question you are answering.

- Carefully and completely fill in the space corresponding to the answer you select for each question. Fill the space with a dark mark so that you cannot see the letter inside the space. Light or partial marks may not be read by the scoring machine. See the example of proper and improper answer marks below.

- Erase all stray marks. If you change an answer, be sure that you completely erase the old answer before marking your new answer. Incomplete erasures may be read as intended answers.

Example: Sample Answer

What city is the capital of France?   Ⓐ ● Ⓒ Ⓓ Ⓔ   CORRECT ANSWER
                                                                                              PROPERLY MARKED

(A) Rome   Ⓐ Ⓑ Ⓒ Ⓓ Ⓔ
(B) Paris   Ⓐ Ⓑ Ⓒ Ⓓ Ⓔ
(C) London   Ⓐ Ⓑ Ⓒ Ⓓ Ⓔ   IMPROPER MARKS
(D) Cairo   Ⓐ Ⓑ Ⓒ Ⓓ Ⓔ
(E) Oslo   Ⓐ Ⓑ Ⓒ Ⓓ Ⓔ

Do not be concerned that the answer sheet provides spaces for more answers than there are questions in the test.

CLOSE YOUR TEST BOOK AND WAIT FOR FURTHER INSTRUCTIONS FROM THE SUPERVISOR.

The Committee of Examiners for the Computer Science Test of the Graduate Record Examinations, appointed with the advice of the Association for Computing Machinery and the IEEE Computer Society:

Edward Lazowska, University of Washington, Chairman
Allan Borodin, University of Toronto
John Gannon, University of Maryland
James Goodman, University of Wisconsin-Madison
Robert Sedgewick, Princeton University
Jeannette Wing, Carnegie Mellon University

with the assistance of

J. R. Jefferson Wadkins, Educational Testing Service
Steven Anacker, Educational Testing Service

I

NOTE: To ensure the prompt and accurate processing of test results, your cooperation in following these directions is needed. The procedures that follow have been kept to the minimum necessary. They will take a few minutes to complete, but it is essential that you fill in all blanks <u>exactly</u> as directed.

SUBJECT TEST

A. Print and sign your full name in this box:

PRINT: _____
            (LAST)   (FIRST)   (MIDDLE)

SIGN: _____

B. Side 1 of your answer sheet contains areas that will be used to ensure accurate reporting of your test results. It is essential that you carefully enter the requested information.

1 through 5 YOUR NAME, DATE OF BIRTH, SOCIAL SECURITY NUMBER, REGISTRATION NUMBER, and ADDRESS: <u>Print</u> all the information requested in the boxes and then fill in completely the appropriate oval beneath each entry.

- For date of birth, be sure to enter a zero before a single digit (e.g., if you were born on the third day of the month, you would enter "03" for the day). Use the last two digits of the year of your birth (for 1966, enter 66).

- Copy the registration number from your admission ticket.

6 TITLE CODE: Copy the numbers shown below and fill in completely the appropriate spaces beneath each entry as shown. When you have completed item 6, check to be sure it is identical to the illustration below.

6. TITLE CODE
2 9 3 1 9

7 TEST NAME: Copy *Computer Science* in the box.

FORM CODE: Copy GR 9129 in the box.

8 TEST BOOK SERIAL NUMBER: Copy the serial number of your test book in the box. It is printed in red at the upper right on the front cover of your test book.

9 <u>Print</u> the requested information and enter the test center number in the boxes.

10 CERTIFICATION STATEMENT: In the boxed area, <u>WRITE</u> (do not print) the following statement: "I certify that I am the person whose name appears on this answer sheet. I also agree not to disclose the contents of the test I am taking today to anyone." Sign and date where indicated.

C. WHEN YOU HAVE FINISHED THESE INSTRUCTIONS, PLEASE TURN YOUR ANSWER SHEET OVER AND SIGN YOUR NAME IN THE BOX EXACTLY AS YOU DID FOR ITEM 10.

When you have finished, wait for further instructions from the supervisor. DO NOT OPEN YOUR TEST BOOK UNTIL YOU ARE TOLD TO DO SO.

GRADUATE RECORD EXAMINATIONS®-GRE®-SUBJECT TEST

SIDE 1

Use only a pencil with a soft, black lead (No. 2 or HB) to complete this answer sheet.
Be sure to fill in completely the space that corresponds to your answer choice.
Completely erase any errors or stray marks.

DO NOT USE INK.

1. NAME

Omit spaces, apostrophes, Jr., II, etc.

Last Name (Family or Surname) - first 15 letters

First Name (Given) - first 12 letters

MI

2. DATE OF BIRTH

Month	Day	Year
Jan.		
Feb.		
Mar.		
Apr.		
May		
June		
July		
Aug.		
Sept.		
Oct.		
Nov.		
Dec.		

3. SOCIAL SECURITY NUMBER

4. REGISTRATION NUMBER

5. P.O. Box or Street Address
(first 10 characters only)

Indicate a space in address by leaving a blank box and filling in the corresponding diamond.

6. TITLE CODE

7. TEST NAME:

FORM CODE:

8. TEST BOOK SERIAL NUMBER:

SHADED AREA FOR ETS USE ONLY

9. YOUR NAME:
(Print)

Last Name (Family or Surname)   First Name (Given)   M.I.

MAILING ADDRESS:

P.O. Box or Street Address

City   State or Province

Country   Zip or Postal Code

CENTER:

City   State or Province

Country   Center Number   Room Number

10. CERTIFICATION STATEMENT

SIGNATURE:

DATE: Month   Day   Year

Copyright © 1991 by Educational Testing Service, Princeton, NJ 08541. All rights reserved. Printed in U.S.A.

chw91029   Q1867-06   54074TF21P200e   I.N.275437

SIDE 2

SUBJECT TEST

IF YOU DO <u>NOT</u> WANT THIS ANSWER SHEET TO BE SCORED

If you want to cancel your scores from this administration, complete A and B below. No record of this test will be sent to your designated recipients, and there will be no scores for this test on your GRE record. You will receive confirmation of this cancellation; you will **not** receive scores for this test. Once a score is canceled, it cannot be reinstated.

To cancel your scores from this test administration, you must:

A. fill in both ovals here . . . . ◯ – ◯

B. sign your name in full below:

SIGNATURE:

BE SURE EACH MARK IS DARK AND COMPLETELY FILLS THE INTENDED SPACE AS ILLUSTRATED HERE: ●.
YOU MAY FIND MORE RESPONSE SPACES THAN YOU NEED. IF SO, PLEASE LEAVE THEM BLANK.

1. Ⓐ Ⓑ Ⓒ Ⓓ Ⓔ   41. Ⓐ Ⓑ Ⓒ Ⓓ Ⓔ   81. Ⓐ Ⓑ Ⓒ Ⓓ Ⓔ   121. Ⓐ Ⓑ Ⓒ Ⓓ Ⓔ   161. Ⓐ Ⓑ Ⓒ Ⓓ Ⓔ   201. Ⓐ Ⓑ Ⓒ Ⓓ Ⓔ
2. Ⓐ Ⓑ Ⓒ Ⓓ Ⓔ   42. Ⓐ Ⓑ Ⓒ Ⓓ Ⓔ   82. Ⓐ Ⓑ Ⓒ Ⓓ Ⓔ   122. Ⓐ Ⓑ Ⓒ Ⓓ Ⓔ   162. Ⓐ Ⓑ Ⓒ Ⓓ Ⓔ   202. Ⓐ Ⓑ Ⓒ Ⓓ Ⓔ
3. Ⓐ Ⓑ Ⓒ Ⓓ Ⓔ   43. Ⓐ Ⓑ Ⓒ Ⓓ Ⓔ   83. Ⓐ Ⓑ Ⓒ Ⓓ Ⓔ   123. Ⓐ Ⓑ Ⓒ Ⓓ Ⓔ   163. Ⓐ Ⓑ Ⓒ Ⓓ Ⓔ   203. Ⓐ Ⓑ Ⓒ Ⓓ Ⓔ
4. Ⓐ Ⓑ Ⓒ Ⓓ Ⓔ   44. Ⓐ Ⓑ Ⓒ Ⓓ Ⓔ   84. Ⓐ Ⓑ Ⓒ Ⓓ Ⓔ   124. Ⓐ Ⓑ Ⓒ Ⓓ Ⓔ   164. Ⓐ Ⓑ Ⓒ Ⓓ Ⓔ   204. Ⓐ Ⓑ Ⓒ Ⓓ Ⓔ
5. Ⓐ Ⓑ Ⓒ Ⓓ Ⓔ   45. Ⓐ Ⓑ Ⓒ Ⓓ Ⓔ   85. Ⓐ Ⓑ Ⓒ Ⓓ Ⓔ   125. Ⓐ Ⓑ Ⓒ Ⓓ Ⓔ   165. Ⓐ Ⓑ Ⓒ Ⓓ Ⓔ   205. Ⓐ Ⓑ Ⓒ Ⓓ Ⓔ
6. Ⓐ Ⓑ Ⓒ Ⓓ Ⓔ   46. Ⓐ Ⓑ Ⓒ Ⓓ Ⓔ   86. Ⓐ Ⓑ Ⓒ Ⓓ Ⓔ   126. Ⓐ Ⓑ Ⓒ Ⓓ Ⓔ   166. Ⓐ Ⓑ Ⓒ Ⓓ Ⓔ   206. Ⓐ Ⓑ Ⓒ Ⓓ Ⓔ
7. Ⓐ Ⓑ Ⓒ Ⓓ Ⓔ   47. Ⓐ Ⓑ Ⓒ Ⓓ Ⓔ   87. Ⓐ Ⓑ Ⓒ Ⓓ Ⓔ   127. Ⓐ Ⓑ Ⓒ Ⓓ Ⓔ   167. Ⓐ Ⓑ Ⓒ Ⓓ Ⓔ   207. Ⓐ Ⓑ Ⓒ Ⓓ Ⓔ
8. Ⓐ Ⓑ Ⓒ Ⓓ Ⓔ   48. Ⓐ Ⓑ Ⓒ Ⓓ Ⓔ   88. Ⓐ Ⓑ Ⓒ Ⓓ Ⓔ   128. Ⓐ Ⓑ Ⓒ Ⓓ Ⓔ   168. Ⓐ Ⓑ Ⓒ Ⓓ Ⓔ   208. Ⓐ Ⓑ Ⓒ Ⓓ Ⓔ
9. Ⓐ Ⓑ Ⓒ Ⓓ Ⓔ   49. Ⓐ Ⓑ Ⓒ Ⓓ Ⓔ   89. Ⓐ Ⓑ Ⓒ Ⓓ Ⓔ   129. Ⓐ Ⓑ Ⓒ Ⓓ Ⓔ   169. Ⓐ Ⓑ Ⓒ Ⓓ Ⓔ   209. Ⓐ Ⓑ Ⓒ Ⓓ Ⓔ
10. Ⓐ Ⓑ Ⓒ Ⓓ Ⓔ   50. Ⓐ Ⓑ Ⓒ Ⓓ Ⓔ   90. Ⓐ Ⓑ Ⓒ Ⓓ Ⓔ   130. Ⓐ Ⓑ Ⓒ Ⓓ Ⓔ   170. Ⓐ Ⓑ Ⓒ Ⓓ Ⓔ   210. Ⓐ Ⓑ Ⓒ Ⓓ Ⓔ
11. Ⓐ Ⓑ Ⓒ Ⓓ Ⓔ   51. Ⓐ Ⓑ Ⓒ Ⓓ Ⓔ   91. Ⓐ Ⓑ Ⓒ Ⓓ Ⓔ   131. Ⓐ Ⓑ Ⓒ Ⓓ Ⓔ   171. Ⓐ Ⓑ Ⓒ Ⓓ Ⓔ   211. Ⓐ Ⓑ Ⓒ Ⓓ Ⓔ
12. Ⓐ Ⓑ Ⓒ Ⓓ Ⓔ   52. Ⓐ Ⓑ Ⓒ Ⓓ Ⓔ   92. Ⓐ Ⓑ Ⓒ Ⓓ Ⓔ   132. Ⓐ Ⓑ Ⓒ Ⓓ Ⓔ   172. Ⓐ Ⓑ Ⓒ Ⓓ Ⓔ   212. Ⓐ Ⓑ Ⓒ Ⓓ Ⓔ
13. Ⓐ Ⓑ Ⓒ Ⓓ Ⓔ   53. Ⓐ Ⓑ Ⓒ Ⓓ Ⓔ   93. Ⓐ Ⓑ Ⓒ Ⓓ Ⓔ   133. Ⓐ Ⓑ Ⓒ Ⓓ Ⓔ   173. Ⓐ Ⓑ Ⓒ Ⓓ Ⓔ   213. Ⓐ Ⓑ Ⓒ Ⓓ Ⓔ
14. Ⓐ Ⓑ Ⓒ Ⓓ Ⓔ   54. Ⓐ Ⓑ Ⓒ Ⓓ Ⓔ   94. Ⓐ Ⓑ Ⓒ Ⓓ Ⓔ   134. Ⓐ Ⓑ Ⓒ Ⓓ Ⓔ   174. Ⓐ Ⓑ Ⓒ Ⓓ Ⓔ   214. Ⓐ Ⓑ Ⓒ Ⓓ Ⓔ
15. Ⓐ Ⓑ Ⓒ Ⓓ Ⓔ   55. Ⓐ Ⓑ Ⓒ Ⓓ Ⓔ   95. Ⓐ Ⓑ Ⓒ Ⓓ Ⓔ   135. Ⓐ Ⓑ Ⓒ Ⓓ Ⓔ   175. Ⓐ Ⓑ Ⓒ Ⓓ Ⓔ   215. Ⓐ Ⓑ Ⓒ Ⓓ Ⓔ
16. Ⓐ Ⓑ Ⓒ Ⓓ Ⓔ   56. Ⓐ Ⓑ Ⓒ Ⓓ Ⓔ   96. Ⓐ Ⓑ Ⓒ Ⓓ Ⓔ   136. Ⓐ Ⓑ Ⓒ Ⓓ Ⓔ   176. Ⓐ Ⓑ Ⓒ Ⓓ Ⓔ   216. Ⓐ Ⓑ Ⓒ Ⓓ Ⓔ
17. Ⓐ Ⓑ Ⓒ Ⓓ Ⓔ   57. Ⓐ Ⓑ Ⓒ Ⓓ Ⓔ   97. Ⓐ Ⓑ Ⓒ Ⓓ Ⓔ   137. Ⓐ Ⓑ Ⓒ Ⓓ Ⓔ   177. Ⓐ Ⓑ Ⓒ Ⓓ Ⓔ   217. Ⓐ Ⓑ Ⓒ Ⓓ Ⓔ
18. Ⓐ Ⓑ Ⓒ Ⓓ Ⓔ   58. Ⓐ Ⓑ Ⓒ Ⓓ Ⓔ   98. Ⓐ Ⓑ Ⓒ Ⓓ Ⓔ   138. Ⓐ Ⓑ Ⓒ Ⓓ Ⓔ   178. Ⓐ Ⓑ Ⓒ Ⓓ Ⓔ   218. Ⓐ Ⓑ Ⓒ Ⓓ Ⓔ
19. Ⓐ Ⓑ Ⓒ Ⓓ Ⓔ   59. Ⓐ Ⓑ Ⓒ Ⓓ Ⓔ   99. Ⓐ Ⓑ Ⓒ Ⓓ Ⓔ   139. Ⓐ Ⓑ Ⓒ Ⓓ Ⓔ   179. Ⓐ Ⓑ Ⓒ Ⓓ Ⓔ   219. Ⓐ Ⓑ Ⓒ Ⓓ Ⓔ
20. Ⓐ Ⓑ Ⓒ Ⓓ Ⓔ   60. Ⓐ Ⓑ Ⓒ Ⓓ Ⓔ   100. Ⓐ Ⓑ Ⓒ Ⓓ Ⓔ   140. Ⓐ Ⓑ Ⓒ Ⓓ Ⓔ   180. Ⓐ Ⓑ Ⓒ Ⓓ Ⓔ   220. Ⓐ Ⓑ Ⓒ Ⓓ Ⓔ
21. Ⓐ Ⓑ Ⓒ Ⓓ Ⓔ   61. Ⓐ Ⓑ Ⓒ Ⓓ Ⓔ   101. Ⓐ Ⓑ Ⓒ Ⓓ Ⓔ   141. Ⓐ Ⓑ Ⓒ Ⓓ Ⓔ   181. Ⓐ Ⓑ Ⓒ Ⓓ Ⓔ   221. Ⓐ Ⓑ Ⓒ Ⓓ Ⓔ
22. Ⓐ Ⓑ Ⓒ Ⓓ Ⓔ   62. Ⓐ Ⓑ Ⓒ Ⓓ Ⓔ   102. Ⓐ Ⓑ Ⓒ Ⓓ Ⓔ   142. Ⓐ Ⓑ Ⓒ Ⓓ Ⓔ   182. Ⓐ Ⓑ Ⓒ Ⓓ Ⓔ   222. Ⓐ Ⓑ Ⓒ Ⓓ Ⓔ
23. Ⓐ Ⓑ Ⓒ Ⓓ Ⓔ   63. Ⓐ Ⓑ Ⓒ Ⓓ Ⓔ   103. Ⓐ Ⓑ Ⓒ Ⓓ Ⓔ   143. Ⓐ Ⓑ Ⓒ Ⓓ Ⓔ   183. Ⓐ Ⓑ Ⓒ Ⓓ Ⓔ   223. Ⓐ Ⓑ Ⓒ Ⓓ Ⓔ
24. Ⓐ Ⓑ Ⓒ Ⓓ Ⓔ   64. Ⓐ Ⓑ Ⓒ Ⓓ Ⓔ   104. Ⓐ Ⓑ Ⓒ Ⓓ Ⓔ   144. Ⓐ Ⓑ Ⓒ Ⓓ Ⓔ   184. Ⓐ Ⓑ Ⓒ Ⓓ Ⓔ   224. Ⓐ Ⓑ Ⓒ Ⓓ Ⓔ
25. Ⓐ Ⓑ Ⓒ Ⓓ Ⓔ   65. Ⓐ Ⓑ Ⓒ Ⓓ Ⓔ   105. Ⓐ Ⓑ Ⓒ Ⓓ Ⓔ   145. Ⓐ Ⓑ Ⓒ Ⓓ Ⓔ   185. Ⓐ Ⓑ Ⓒ Ⓓ Ⓔ   225. Ⓐ Ⓑ Ⓒ Ⓓ Ⓔ
26. Ⓐ Ⓑ Ⓒ Ⓓ Ⓔ   66. Ⓐ Ⓑ Ⓒ Ⓓ Ⓔ   106. Ⓐ Ⓑ Ⓒ Ⓓ Ⓔ   146. Ⓐ Ⓑ Ⓒ Ⓓ Ⓔ   186. Ⓐ Ⓑ Ⓒ Ⓓ Ⓔ   226. Ⓐ Ⓑ Ⓒ Ⓓ Ⓔ
27. Ⓐ Ⓑ Ⓒ Ⓓ Ⓔ   67. Ⓐ Ⓑ Ⓒ Ⓓ Ⓔ   107. Ⓐ Ⓑ Ⓒ Ⓓ Ⓔ   147. Ⓐ Ⓑ Ⓒ Ⓓ Ⓔ   187. Ⓐ Ⓑ Ⓒ Ⓓ Ⓔ   227. Ⓐ Ⓑ Ⓒ Ⓓ Ⓔ
28. Ⓐ Ⓑ Ⓒ Ⓓ Ⓔ   68. Ⓐ Ⓑ Ⓒ Ⓓ Ⓔ   108. Ⓐ Ⓑ Ⓒ Ⓓ Ⓔ   148. Ⓐ Ⓑ Ⓒ Ⓓ Ⓔ   188. Ⓐ Ⓑ Ⓒ Ⓓ Ⓔ   228. Ⓐ Ⓑ Ⓒ Ⓓ Ⓔ
29. Ⓐ Ⓑ Ⓒ Ⓓ Ⓔ   69. Ⓐ Ⓑ Ⓒ Ⓓ Ⓔ   109. Ⓐ Ⓑ Ⓒ Ⓓ Ⓔ   149. Ⓐ Ⓑ Ⓒ Ⓓ Ⓔ   189. Ⓐ Ⓑ Ⓒ Ⓓ Ⓔ   229. Ⓐ Ⓑ Ⓒ Ⓓ Ⓔ
30. Ⓐ Ⓑ Ⓒ Ⓓ Ⓔ   70. Ⓐ Ⓑ Ⓒ Ⓓ Ⓔ   110. Ⓐ Ⓑ Ⓒ Ⓓ Ⓔ   150. Ⓐ Ⓑ Ⓒ Ⓓ Ⓔ   190. Ⓐ Ⓑ Ⓒ Ⓓ Ⓔ   230. Ⓐ Ⓑ Ⓒ Ⓓ Ⓔ
31. Ⓐ Ⓑ Ⓒ Ⓓ Ⓔ   71. Ⓐ Ⓑ Ⓒ Ⓓ Ⓔ   111. Ⓐ Ⓑ Ⓒ Ⓓ Ⓔ   151. Ⓐ Ⓑ Ⓒ Ⓓ Ⓔ   191. Ⓐ Ⓑ Ⓒ Ⓓ Ⓔ   231. Ⓐ Ⓑ Ⓒ Ⓓ Ⓔ
32. Ⓐ Ⓑ Ⓒ Ⓓ Ⓔ   72. Ⓐ Ⓑ Ⓒ Ⓓ Ⓔ   112. Ⓐ Ⓑ Ⓒ Ⓓ Ⓔ   152. Ⓐ Ⓑ Ⓒ Ⓓ Ⓔ   192. Ⓐ Ⓑ Ⓒ Ⓓ Ⓔ   232. Ⓐ Ⓑ Ⓒ Ⓓ Ⓔ
33. Ⓐ Ⓑ Ⓒ Ⓓ Ⓔ   73. Ⓐ Ⓑ Ⓒ Ⓓ Ⓔ   113. Ⓐ Ⓑ Ⓒ Ⓓ Ⓔ   153. Ⓐ Ⓑ Ⓒ Ⓓ Ⓔ   193. Ⓐ Ⓑ Ⓒ Ⓓ Ⓔ   233. Ⓐ Ⓑ Ⓒ Ⓓ Ⓔ
34. Ⓐ Ⓑ Ⓒ Ⓓ Ⓔ   74. Ⓐ Ⓑ Ⓒ Ⓓ Ⓔ   114. Ⓐ Ⓑ Ⓒ Ⓓ Ⓔ   154. Ⓐ Ⓑ Ⓒ Ⓓ Ⓔ   194. Ⓐ Ⓑ Ⓒ Ⓓ Ⓔ   234. Ⓐ Ⓑ Ⓒ Ⓓ Ⓔ
35. Ⓐ Ⓑ Ⓒ Ⓓ Ⓔ   75. Ⓐ Ⓑ Ⓒ Ⓓ Ⓔ   115. Ⓐ Ⓑ Ⓒ Ⓓ Ⓔ   155. Ⓐ Ⓑ Ⓒ Ⓓ Ⓔ   195. Ⓐ Ⓑ Ⓒ Ⓓ Ⓔ   235. Ⓐ Ⓑ Ⓒ Ⓓ Ⓔ
36. Ⓐ Ⓑ Ⓒ Ⓓ Ⓔ   76. Ⓐ Ⓑ Ⓒ Ⓓ Ⓔ   116. Ⓐ Ⓑ Ⓒ Ⓓ Ⓔ   156. Ⓐ Ⓑ Ⓒ Ⓓ Ⓔ   196. Ⓐ Ⓑ Ⓒ Ⓓ Ⓔ   236. Ⓐ Ⓑ Ⓒ Ⓓ Ⓔ
37. Ⓐ Ⓑ Ⓒ Ⓓ Ⓔ   77. Ⓐ Ⓑ Ⓒ Ⓓ Ⓔ   117. Ⓐ Ⓑ Ⓒ Ⓓ Ⓔ   157. Ⓐ Ⓑ Ⓒ Ⓓ Ⓔ   197. Ⓐ Ⓑ Ⓒ Ⓓ Ⓔ   237. Ⓐ Ⓑ Ⓒ Ⓓ Ⓔ
38. Ⓐ Ⓑ Ⓒ Ⓓ Ⓔ   78. Ⓐ Ⓑ Ⓒ Ⓓ Ⓔ   118. Ⓐ Ⓑ Ⓒ Ⓓ Ⓔ   158. Ⓐ Ⓑ Ⓒ Ⓓ Ⓔ   198. Ⓐ Ⓑ Ⓒ Ⓓ Ⓔ   238. Ⓐ Ⓑ Ⓒ Ⓓ Ⓔ
39. Ⓐ Ⓑ Ⓒ Ⓓ Ⓔ   79. Ⓐ Ⓑ Ⓒ Ⓓ Ⓔ   119. Ⓐ Ⓑ Ⓒ Ⓓ Ⓔ   159. Ⓐ Ⓑ Ⓒ Ⓓ Ⓔ   199. Ⓐ Ⓑ Ⓒ Ⓓ Ⓔ   239. Ⓐ Ⓑ Ⓒ Ⓓ Ⓔ
40. Ⓐ Ⓑ Ⓒ Ⓓ Ⓔ   80. Ⓐ Ⓑ Ⓒ Ⓓ Ⓔ   120. Ⓐ Ⓑ Ⓒ Ⓓ Ⓔ   160. Ⓐ Ⓑ Ⓒ Ⓓ Ⓔ   200. Ⓐ Ⓑ Ⓒ Ⓓ Ⓔ   240. Ⓐ Ⓑ Ⓒ Ⓓ Ⓔ

FOR ETS USE ONLY	TR	TW	TF3	TCS	1R	1W	1FS	1CS	2R	2W	2FS	2CS	3R	3W	3FS	3CS

GRADUATE RECORD EXAMINATIONS®-GRE®-SUBJECT TEST

SIDE 1

Use only a pencil with a soft, black lead (No. 2 or HB) to complete this answer sheet.
Be sure to fill in completely the space that corresponds to your answer choice.
Completely erase any errors or stray marks.

DO <u>NOT</u> USE INK.

1. NAME

Omit spaces, apostrophes, Jr., II, etc.

Last Name (Family or Surname) - first 15 letters

First Name (Given) - first 12 letters

MI

2. DATE OF BIRTH

Month	Day	Year
○ Jan.		
○ Feb.		
○ Mar.		
○ Apr.		
○ May		
○ June		
○ July		
○ Aug.		
○ Sept.		
○ Oct.		
○ Nov.		
○ Dec.		

3. SOCIAL SECURITY NUMBER

4. REGISTRATION NUMBER

5. P.O. Box or Street Address (first 10 characters only)

Indicate a space in address by leaving a blank box and filling in the corresponding diamond.

6. TITLE CODE

7. TEST NAME:

FORM CODE:

8. TEST BOOK SERIAL NUMBER:

SHADED AREA FOR ETS USE ONLY

9. YOUR NAME:

Last Name (Family or Surname)   First Name (Given)   M.I.

MAILING ADDRESS:
(Print)

P.O. Box or Street Address

City   State or Province

Country   Zip or Postal Code

CENTER:

City   State or Province

Country   Center Number   Room Number

10. CERTIFICATION STATEMENT

SIGNATURE:

DATE: _____ / _____ / _____
           Month   Day   Year

chw91029   Q1867-06   54074TF21P200e   I.N.275437

Ⓔ Copyright © 1991 by Educational Testing Service, Princeton, NJ 08541. All rights reserved. Printed in U.S.A.

SIDE 2

SUBJECT TEST

IF YOU DO NOT WANT THIS ANSWER SHEET TO BE SCORED

If you want to cancel your scores from this administration, complete A and B below. No record of this test will be sent to your designated recipients, and there will be no scores for this test on your GRE record. You will receive confirmation of this cancellation; you will **not** receive scores for this test. Once a score is canceled, it cannot be reinstated.

To cancel your scores from this test administration, you must:

A. fill in both ovals here . . . . ○ – ○

B. sign your name in full below:

SIGNATURE:

_____

BE SURE EACH MARK IS DARK AND COMPLETELY FILLS THE INTENDED SPACE AS ILLUSTRATED HERE: ●.
YOU MAY FIND MORE RESPONSE SPACES THAN YOU NEED. IF SO, PLEASE LEAVE THEM BLANK.

1. Ⓐ Ⓑ Ⓒ Ⓓ Ⓔ	41. Ⓐ Ⓑ Ⓒ Ⓓ Ⓔ	81. Ⓐ Ⓑ Ⓒ Ⓓ Ⓔ	121. Ⓐ Ⓑ Ⓒ Ⓓ Ⓔ	161. Ⓐ Ⓑ Ⓒ Ⓓ Ⓔ	201. Ⓐ Ⓑ Ⓒ Ⓓ Ⓔ
2. Ⓐ Ⓑ Ⓒ Ⓓ Ⓔ	42. Ⓐ Ⓑ Ⓒ Ⓓ Ⓔ	82. Ⓐ Ⓑ Ⓒ Ⓓ Ⓔ	122. Ⓐ Ⓑ Ⓒ Ⓓ Ⓔ	162. Ⓐ Ⓑ Ⓒ Ⓓ Ⓔ	202. Ⓐ Ⓑ Ⓒ Ⓓ Ⓔ
3. Ⓐ Ⓑ Ⓒ Ⓓ Ⓔ	43. Ⓐ Ⓑ Ⓒ Ⓓ Ⓔ	83. Ⓐ Ⓑ Ⓒ Ⓓ Ⓔ	123. Ⓐ Ⓑ Ⓒ Ⓓ Ⓔ	163. Ⓐ Ⓑ Ⓒ Ⓓ Ⓔ	203. Ⓐ Ⓑ Ⓒ Ⓓ Ⓔ
4. Ⓐ Ⓑ Ⓒ Ⓓ Ⓔ	44. Ⓐ Ⓑ Ⓒ Ⓓ Ⓔ	84. Ⓐ Ⓑ Ⓒ Ⓓ Ⓔ	124. Ⓐ Ⓑ Ⓒ Ⓓ Ⓔ	164. Ⓐ Ⓑ Ⓒ Ⓓ Ⓔ	204. Ⓐ Ⓑ Ⓒ Ⓓ Ⓔ
5. Ⓐ Ⓑ Ⓒ Ⓓ Ⓔ	45. Ⓐ Ⓑ Ⓒ Ⓓ Ⓔ	85. Ⓐ Ⓑ Ⓒ Ⓓ Ⓔ	125. Ⓐ Ⓑ Ⓒ Ⓓ Ⓔ	165. Ⓐ Ⓑ Ⓒ Ⓓ Ⓔ	205. Ⓐ Ⓑ Ⓒ Ⓓ Ⓔ
6. Ⓐ Ⓑ Ⓒ Ⓓ Ⓔ	46. Ⓐ Ⓑ Ⓒ Ⓓ Ⓔ	86. Ⓐ Ⓑ Ⓒ Ⓓ Ⓔ	126. Ⓐ Ⓑ Ⓒ Ⓓ Ⓔ	166. Ⓐ Ⓑ Ⓒ Ⓓ Ⓔ	206. Ⓐ Ⓑ Ⓒ Ⓓ Ⓔ
7. Ⓐ Ⓑ Ⓒ Ⓓ Ⓔ	47. Ⓐ Ⓑ Ⓒ Ⓓ Ⓔ	87. Ⓐ Ⓑ Ⓒ Ⓓ Ⓔ	127. Ⓐ Ⓑ Ⓒ Ⓓ Ⓔ	167. Ⓐ Ⓑ Ⓒ Ⓓ Ⓔ	207. Ⓐ Ⓑ Ⓒ Ⓓ Ⓔ
8. Ⓐ Ⓑ Ⓒ Ⓓ Ⓔ	48. Ⓐ Ⓑ Ⓒ Ⓓ Ⓔ	88. Ⓐ Ⓑ Ⓒ Ⓓ Ⓔ	128. Ⓐ Ⓑ Ⓒ Ⓓ Ⓔ	168. Ⓐ Ⓑ Ⓒ Ⓓ Ⓔ	208. Ⓐ Ⓑ Ⓒ Ⓓ Ⓔ
9. Ⓐ Ⓑ Ⓒ Ⓓ Ⓔ	49. Ⓐ Ⓑ Ⓒ Ⓓ Ⓔ	89. Ⓐ Ⓑ Ⓒ Ⓓ Ⓔ	129. Ⓐ Ⓑ Ⓒ Ⓓ Ⓔ	169. Ⓐ Ⓑ Ⓒ Ⓓ Ⓔ	209. Ⓐ Ⓑ Ⓒ Ⓓ Ⓔ
10. Ⓐ Ⓑ Ⓒ Ⓓ Ⓔ	50. Ⓐ Ⓑ Ⓒ Ⓓ Ⓔ	90. Ⓐ Ⓑ Ⓒ Ⓓ Ⓔ	130. Ⓐ Ⓑ Ⓒ Ⓓ Ⓔ	170. Ⓐ Ⓑ Ⓒ Ⓓ Ⓔ	210. Ⓐ Ⓑ Ⓒ Ⓓ Ⓔ
11. Ⓐ Ⓑ Ⓒ Ⓓ Ⓔ	51. Ⓐ Ⓑ Ⓒ Ⓓ Ⓔ	91. Ⓐ Ⓑ Ⓒ Ⓓ Ⓔ	131. Ⓐ Ⓑ Ⓒ Ⓓ Ⓔ	171. Ⓐ Ⓑ Ⓒ Ⓓ Ⓔ	211. Ⓐ Ⓑ Ⓒ Ⓓ Ⓔ
12. Ⓐ Ⓑ Ⓒ Ⓓ Ⓔ	52. Ⓐ Ⓑ Ⓒ Ⓓ Ⓔ	92. Ⓐ Ⓑ Ⓒ Ⓓ Ⓔ	132. Ⓐ Ⓑ Ⓒ Ⓓ Ⓔ	172. Ⓐ Ⓑ Ⓒ Ⓓ Ⓔ	212. Ⓐ Ⓑ Ⓒ Ⓓ Ⓔ
13. Ⓐ Ⓑ Ⓒ Ⓓ Ⓔ	53. Ⓐ Ⓑ Ⓒ Ⓓ Ⓔ	93. Ⓐ Ⓑ Ⓒ Ⓓ Ⓔ	133. Ⓐ Ⓑ Ⓒ Ⓓ Ⓔ	173. Ⓐ Ⓑ Ⓒ Ⓓ Ⓔ	213. Ⓐ Ⓑ Ⓒ Ⓓ Ⓔ
14. Ⓐ Ⓑ Ⓒ Ⓓ Ⓔ	54. Ⓐ Ⓑ Ⓒ Ⓓ Ⓔ	94. Ⓐ Ⓑ Ⓒ Ⓓ Ⓔ	134. Ⓐ Ⓑ Ⓒ Ⓓ Ⓔ	174. Ⓐ Ⓑ Ⓒ Ⓓ Ⓔ	214. Ⓐ Ⓑ Ⓒ Ⓓ Ⓔ
15. Ⓐ Ⓑ Ⓒ Ⓓ Ⓔ	55. Ⓐ Ⓑ Ⓒ Ⓓ Ⓔ	95. Ⓐ Ⓑ Ⓒ Ⓓ Ⓔ	135. Ⓐ Ⓑ Ⓒ Ⓓ Ⓔ	175. Ⓐ Ⓑ Ⓒ Ⓓ Ⓔ	215. Ⓐ Ⓑ Ⓒ Ⓓ Ⓔ
16. Ⓐ Ⓑ Ⓒ Ⓓ Ⓔ	56. Ⓐ Ⓑ Ⓒ Ⓓ Ⓔ	96. Ⓐ Ⓑ Ⓒ Ⓓ Ⓔ	136. Ⓐ Ⓑ Ⓒ Ⓓ Ⓔ	176. Ⓐ Ⓑ Ⓒ Ⓓ Ⓔ	216. Ⓐ Ⓑ Ⓒ Ⓓ Ⓔ
17. Ⓐ Ⓑ Ⓒ Ⓓ Ⓔ	57. Ⓐ Ⓑ Ⓒ Ⓓ Ⓔ	97. Ⓐ Ⓑ Ⓒ Ⓓ Ⓔ	137. Ⓐ Ⓑ Ⓒ Ⓓ Ⓔ	177. Ⓐ Ⓑ Ⓒ Ⓓ Ⓔ	217. Ⓐ Ⓑ Ⓒ Ⓓ Ⓔ
18. Ⓐ Ⓑ Ⓒ Ⓓ Ⓔ	58. Ⓐ Ⓑ Ⓒ Ⓓ Ⓔ	98. Ⓐ Ⓑ Ⓒ Ⓓ Ⓔ	138. Ⓐ Ⓑ Ⓒ Ⓓ Ⓔ	178. Ⓐ Ⓑ Ⓒ Ⓓ Ⓔ	218. Ⓐ Ⓑ Ⓒ Ⓓ Ⓔ
19. Ⓐ Ⓑ Ⓒ Ⓓ Ⓔ	59. Ⓐ Ⓑ Ⓒ Ⓓ Ⓔ	99. Ⓐ Ⓑ Ⓒ Ⓓ Ⓔ	139. Ⓐ Ⓑ Ⓒ Ⓓ Ⓔ	179. Ⓐ Ⓑ Ⓒ Ⓓ Ⓔ	219. Ⓐ Ⓑ Ⓒ Ⓓ Ⓔ
20. Ⓐ Ⓑ Ⓒ Ⓓ Ⓔ	60. Ⓐ Ⓑ Ⓒ Ⓓ Ⓔ	100. Ⓐ Ⓑ Ⓒ Ⓓ Ⓔ	140. Ⓐ Ⓑ Ⓒ Ⓓ Ⓔ	180. Ⓐ Ⓑ Ⓒ Ⓓ Ⓔ	220. Ⓐ Ⓑ Ⓒ Ⓓ Ⓔ
21. Ⓐ Ⓑ Ⓒ Ⓓ Ⓔ	61. Ⓐ Ⓑ Ⓒ Ⓓ Ⓔ	101. Ⓐ Ⓑ Ⓒ Ⓓ Ⓔ	141. Ⓐ Ⓑ Ⓒ Ⓓ Ⓔ	181. Ⓐ Ⓑ Ⓒ Ⓓ Ⓔ	221. Ⓐ Ⓑ Ⓒ Ⓓ Ⓔ
22. Ⓐ Ⓑ Ⓒ Ⓓ Ⓔ	62. Ⓐ Ⓑ Ⓒ Ⓓ Ⓔ	102. Ⓐ Ⓑ Ⓒ Ⓓ Ⓔ	142. Ⓐ Ⓑ Ⓒ Ⓓ Ⓔ	182. Ⓐ Ⓑ Ⓒ Ⓓ Ⓔ	222. Ⓐ Ⓑ Ⓒ Ⓓ Ⓔ
23. Ⓐ Ⓑ Ⓒ Ⓓ Ⓔ	63. Ⓐ Ⓑ Ⓒ Ⓓ Ⓔ	103. Ⓐ Ⓑ Ⓒ Ⓓ Ⓔ	143. Ⓐ Ⓑ Ⓒ Ⓓ Ⓔ	183. Ⓐ Ⓑ Ⓒ Ⓓ Ⓔ	223. Ⓐ Ⓑ Ⓒ Ⓓ Ⓔ
24. Ⓐ Ⓑ Ⓒ Ⓓ Ⓔ	64. Ⓐ Ⓑ Ⓒ Ⓓ Ⓔ	104. Ⓐ Ⓑ Ⓒ Ⓓ Ⓔ	144. Ⓐ Ⓑ Ⓒ Ⓓ Ⓔ	184. Ⓐ Ⓑ Ⓒ Ⓓ Ⓔ	224. Ⓐ Ⓑ Ⓒ Ⓓ Ⓔ
25. Ⓐ Ⓑ Ⓒ Ⓓ Ⓔ	65. Ⓐ Ⓑ Ⓒ Ⓓ Ⓔ	105. Ⓐ Ⓑ Ⓒ Ⓓ Ⓔ	145. Ⓐ Ⓑ Ⓒ Ⓓ Ⓔ	185. Ⓐ Ⓑ Ⓒ Ⓓ Ⓔ	225. Ⓐ Ⓑ Ⓒ Ⓓ Ⓔ
26. Ⓐ Ⓑ Ⓒ Ⓓ Ⓔ	66. Ⓐ Ⓑ Ⓒ Ⓓ Ⓔ	106. Ⓐ Ⓑ Ⓒ Ⓓ Ⓔ	146. Ⓐ Ⓑ Ⓒ Ⓓ Ⓔ	186. Ⓐ Ⓑ Ⓒ Ⓓ Ⓔ	226. Ⓐ Ⓑ Ⓒ Ⓓ Ⓔ
27. Ⓐ Ⓑ Ⓒ Ⓓ Ⓔ	67. Ⓐ Ⓑ Ⓒ Ⓓ Ⓔ	107. Ⓐ Ⓑ Ⓒ Ⓓ Ⓔ	147. Ⓐ Ⓑ Ⓒ Ⓓ Ⓔ	187. Ⓐ Ⓑ Ⓒ Ⓓ Ⓔ	227. Ⓐ Ⓑ Ⓒ Ⓓ Ⓔ
28. Ⓐ Ⓑ Ⓒ Ⓓ Ⓔ	68. Ⓐ Ⓑ Ⓒ Ⓓ Ⓔ	108. Ⓐ Ⓑ Ⓒ Ⓓ Ⓔ	148. Ⓐ Ⓑ Ⓒ Ⓓ Ⓔ	188. Ⓐ Ⓑ Ⓒ Ⓓ Ⓔ	228. Ⓐ Ⓑ Ⓒ Ⓓ Ⓔ
29. Ⓐ Ⓑ Ⓒ Ⓓ Ⓔ	69. Ⓐ Ⓑ Ⓒ Ⓓ Ⓔ	109. Ⓐ Ⓑ Ⓒ Ⓓ Ⓔ	149. Ⓐ Ⓑ Ⓒ Ⓓ Ⓔ	189. Ⓐ Ⓑ Ⓒ Ⓓ Ⓔ	229. Ⓐ Ⓑ Ⓒ Ⓓ Ⓔ
30. Ⓐ Ⓑ Ⓒ Ⓓ Ⓔ	70. Ⓐ Ⓑ Ⓒ Ⓓ Ⓔ	110. Ⓐ Ⓑ Ⓒ Ⓓ Ⓔ	150. Ⓐ Ⓑ Ⓒ Ⓓ Ⓔ	190. Ⓐ Ⓑ Ⓒ Ⓓ Ⓔ	230. Ⓐ Ⓑ Ⓒ Ⓓ Ⓔ
31. Ⓐ Ⓑ Ⓒ Ⓓ Ⓔ	71. Ⓐ Ⓑ Ⓒ Ⓓ Ⓔ	111. Ⓐ Ⓑ Ⓒ Ⓓ Ⓔ	151. Ⓐ Ⓑ Ⓒ Ⓓ Ⓔ	191. Ⓐ Ⓑ Ⓒ Ⓓ Ⓔ	231. Ⓐ Ⓑ Ⓒ Ⓓ Ⓔ
32. Ⓐ Ⓑ Ⓒ Ⓓ Ⓔ	72. Ⓐ Ⓑ Ⓒ Ⓓ Ⓔ	112. Ⓐ Ⓑ Ⓒ Ⓓ Ⓔ	152. Ⓐ Ⓑ Ⓒ Ⓓ Ⓔ	192. Ⓐ Ⓑ Ⓒ Ⓓ Ⓔ	232. Ⓐ Ⓑ Ⓒ Ⓓ Ⓔ
33. Ⓐ Ⓑ Ⓒ Ⓓ Ⓔ	73. Ⓐ Ⓑ Ⓒ Ⓓ Ⓔ	113. Ⓐ Ⓑ Ⓒ Ⓓ Ⓔ	153. Ⓐ Ⓑ Ⓒ Ⓓ Ⓔ	193. Ⓐ Ⓑ Ⓒ Ⓓ Ⓔ	233. Ⓐ Ⓑ Ⓒ Ⓓ Ⓔ
34. Ⓐ Ⓑ Ⓒ Ⓓ Ⓔ	74. Ⓐ Ⓑ Ⓒ Ⓓ Ⓔ	114. Ⓐ Ⓑ Ⓒ Ⓓ Ⓔ	154. Ⓐ Ⓑ Ⓒ Ⓓ Ⓔ	194. Ⓐ Ⓑ Ⓒ Ⓓ Ⓔ	234. Ⓐ Ⓑ Ⓒ Ⓓ Ⓔ
35. Ⓐ Ⓑ Ⓒ Ⓓ Ⓔ	75. Ⓐ Ⓑ Ⓒ Ⓓ Ⓔ	115. Ⓐ Ⓑ Ⓒ Ⓓ Ⓔ	155. Ⓐ Ⓑ Ⓒ Ⓓ Ⓔ	195. Ⓐ Ⓑ Ⓒ Ⓓ Ⓔ	235. Ⓐ Ⓑ Ⓒ Ⓓ Ⓔ
36. Ⓐ Ⓑ Ⓒ Ⓓ Ⓔ	76. Ⓐ Ⓑ Ⓒ Ⓓ Ⓔ	116. Ⓐ Ⓑ Ⓒ Ⓓ Ⓔ	156. Ⓐ Ⓑ Ⓒ Ⓓ Ⓔ	196. Ⓐ Ⓑ Ⓒ Ⓓ Ⓔ	236. Ⓐ Ⓑ Ⓒ Ⓓ Ⓔ
37. Ⓐ Ⓑ Ⓒ Ⓓ Ⓔ	77. Ⓐ Ⓑ Ⓒ Ⓓ Ⓔ	117. Ⓐ Ⓑ Ⓒ Ⓓ Ⓔ	157. Ⓐ Ⓑ Ⓒ Ⓓ Ⓔ	197. Ⓐ Ⓑ Ⓒ Ⓓ Ⓔ	237. Ⓐ Ⓑ Ⓒ Ⓓ Ⓔ
38. Ⓐ Ⓑ Ⓒ Ⓓ Ⓔ	78. Ⓐ Ⓑ Ⓒ Ⓓ Ⓔ	118. Ⓐ Ⓑ Ⓒ Ⓓ Ⓔ	158. Ⓐ Ⓑ Ⓒ Ⓓ Ⓔ	198. Ⓐ Ⓑ Ⓒ Ⓓ Ⓔ	238. Ⓐ Ⓑ Ⓒ Ⓓ Ⓔ
39. Ⓐ Ⓑ Ⓒ Ⓓ Ⓔ	79. Ⓐ Ⓑ Ⓒ Ⓓ Ⓔ	119. Ⓐ Ⓑ Ⓒ Ⓓ Ⓔ	159. Ⓐ Ⓑ Ⓒ Ⓓ Ⓔ	199. Ⓐ Ⓑ Ⓒ Ⓓ Ⓔ	239. Ⓐ Ⓑ Ⓒ Ⓓ Ⓔ
40. Ⓐ Ⓑ Ⓒ Ⓓ Ⓔ	80. Ⓐ Ⓑ Ⓒ Ⓓ Ⓔ	120. Ⓐ Ⓑ Ⓒ Ⓓ Ⓔ	160. Ⓐ Ⓑ Ⓒ Ⓓ Ⓔ	200. Ⓐ Ⓑ Ⓒ Ⓓ Ⓔ	240. Ⓐ Ⓑ Ⓒ Ⓓ Ⓔ

FOR ETS USE ONLY	TR	TW	TF3	TCS	1R	1W	1FS	1CS	2R	2W	2FS	2CS	3R	3W	3FS	3CS

GRE® PUBLICATIONS ORDER FORM
1991-92

Graduate Record Examinations
Educational Testing Service
P.O. Box 6014
Princeton, NJ 08541-6014

P-60

Item Number	Publication	Price*	No. of Copies	Amount	Total
	Practice Test Books (540-01)				
241245	Practicing to Take the GRE General Test — No. 8	$12.00			
241235	Practicing to Take the GRE General Test — No. 7	10.00			
241241	Practicing to Take the GRE Biology Test — 2nd Edition	11.00			
241242	Practicing to Take the GRE Chemistry Test — 2nd Edition	11.00			
241250	† Practicing to Take the GRE Computer Science Test — 2nd Edition	11.00			
241249	† Practicing to Take the GRE Economics Test — 2nd Edition	11.00			
241236	Practicing to Take the GRE Education Test — 2nd Edition	11.00			
241237	Practicing to Take the GRE Engineering Test — 2nd Edition	11.00			
241227	Practicing to Take the GRE Geology Test	9.00			
241219	Practicing to Take the GRE History Test	9.00			
241243	Practicing to Take the GRE Literature in English Test — 2nd Edition	11.00			
241228	Practicing to Take the GRE Mathematics Test	9.00			
241244	Practicing to Take the GRE Revised Music Test	9.00			
241246	Practicing to Take the GRE Physics Test	9.00			
241234	Practicing to Take the GRE Political Science Test	9.00			
241238	Practicing to Take the GRE Psychology Test — 2nd Edition	11.00			
241229	Practicing to Take the GRE Sociology Test	9.00			
	Software Editions (540-07)				
299623	† Practicing to Take the GRE General Test — No. 7, Apple Macintosh Software Edition Version 2.1	80.00			
299624	† Practicing to Take the GRE General Test — No. 7, IBM Software Edition Version 2.1	80.00			
	Directory of Graduate Programs (540-99)				
252030	† Volume A — Natural Sciences	17.00			
252031	† Volume B — Engineering ● Business	17.00			
252032	† Volume C — Social Sciences ● Education	17.00			
252033	† Volume D — Arts ● Humanities ● Other Fields	17.00			

* **Postage: In North America, U.S. Territories, and APO addresses,** postage and handling to a single address is included in the price of the publication.

    To all other locations (airmail only) for postage and handling to a single address, add $4 for the first book ordered and $2 for each additional book. Add $10 for each software edition ordered.

† Available September 1991

● Allow three to four weeks for delivery.

● Payment should be made by check or money order drawn on a U.S. or Canadian bank, U.S. Postal Money Order, or UNESCO Coupons.

● Orders received without payment or a purchase order will be returned.

TYPE OR PRINT CLEARLY BELOW. DO NOT DETACH THESE MAILING LABELS.

POSTAGE ▶
540-52

Make your remittance payable to **ETS-GRE**.

◀ TOTAL AMOUNT ENCLOSED ▶

ETS use only

Graduate Record Examinations
Educational Testing Service
P.O. Box 6014
Princeton, NJ 08541-6014

TO:_____

_____

_____

Graduate Record Examinations
Educational Testing Service
P.O. Box 6014
Princeton, NJ 08541-6014

TO:_____

_____

_____